"This self-help workbook is an excellent tool to help alleviate bulimia nervosa symptoms. It is also a useful guide for the practitioner who is assisting the patient in his or her quest to overcome an eating disorder. I highly recommend this workbook to sufferers and mental health professionals alike."

—Daniel le Grange, Ph.D., professor and director of the eating disorders program at the University of Chicago

"DBT has taught me how to meditate more effectively throughout the day, regulate my emotions, and tolerate the most uncomfortable and painful of times. I never knew how to ride the rollercoaster of life without resorting to bingeing until DBT helped to change my behavior and my life. Because DBT centers on mindfulness—being in the present moment—and having both acceptance of my condition as well as the willingness to change, I can now show up for my life without resorting to bingeing or other crutches. DBT has changed my life, and I have faith that it can change yours!"

—Sharon, client of coauthor Ellen Astrachan-Fletcher

"At my first dialectical behavior therapy (DBT) skills training session, I found it easier to speak without using vowels than to speak without judgment. I was skeptical, but desperate to have a life without my eating disorder, and once desperation won the battle over skepticism, I was in. Once I was able to chip away at the judgment, I began to think it might be possible there was a way to deal with distress that didn't involve binge-purging. Before DBT, my emotions were something that required treatment. Happy, sad, angry, or glad, if I felt something, bulimia was right there to take me back to a state of numbness. Being able to radically and mindfully accept, without judgment, that I could actually experience an emotion and not have it end with a binge was a fascinating revelation. I still fight with bulimia, but I am armed with the tools of DBT and it's now a battle I have a chance of winning."

—Ilene, client of coauthor Ellen Astrachan-Fletcher

"At first, I was very reluctant to join a DBT group, as I thought that I had control over my eating disorder. However, once I decided to participate in a group, I was hooked. For over two years, I have been involved in DBT. DBT has been a life-altering experience and my commitment has truly helped me to be present and create a life worth living."

—Carissa, client of coauthor Ellen Astrachan-Fletcher

"My commitment to DBT has brought me to an understanding of living in the moment. I now carry the benefits of instinctively knowing how to embrace life in an effective way. It is amazing how the exercises brought me to the awareness of just how little time I am now spending thinking obsessive thoughts about exercise and food!"

—Eileen, client of coauthor Ellen Astrachan-Fletcher

"DBT has given me an appreciation for what I believed to be the most insignificant pieces in life: what is going on around me in the present moment. My eating disorder had taken away the familiarity of the simplest joys in life and had focused my attention to my body, exercise, and food. DBT had helped me refocus my attention to the present moment, rather than the past or future."

—Annie, client of coauthor Ellen Astrachan-Fletcher

The Dialectical Behavior Therapy Skills Workbook

— for —

Bulimia

Using DBT to Break the Cycle and Regain Control of Your Life

ELLEN ASTRACHAN-FLETCHER, PH.D.
MICHAEL MASLAR, PSY.D.

New Harbinger Publications, Inc.

Publisher's Note

This publication is designed to provide accurate and authoritative information in regard to the subject matter covered. It is sold with the understanding that the publisher is not engaged in rendering psychological, financial, legal, or other professional services. If expert assistance or counseling is needed, the services of a competent professional should be sought.

Distributed in Canada by Raincoast Books

Copyright © 2009 by Ellen Astrachan-Fletcher and Michael Maslar
New Harbinger Publications, Inc.
5674 Shattuck Avenue
Oakland, CA 94609
www.newharbinger.com

Portia Nelson, "Autobiography in Five Short Chapters" from *There's a Hole in My Sidewalk*, copyright 1994, reprinted with permission from Beyond Words Publishing.

Acquired by Catharine Sutker; Cover design by Amy Shoup; Text design by Tracy Carlson

Library of Congress Cataloging-in-Publication Data
Astrachan-Fletcher, Ellen.
 The dialectical behavior therapy skills workbook for bulimia : using DBT break the cycle and regain control of your life / Ellen Astrachan-Fletcher and Michael Maslar.
     p. cm.
 Includes bibliographical references.
 ISBN-13: 978-1-57224-619-5 (pbk. : alk. paper)
 ISBN-10: 1-57224-619-7 (pbk. : alk. paper)
 1. Bulimia--Treatment--Popular works. 2. Dialectical behavior therapy--Popular works. 3. Bulimia--Patients--Life skills guides. I.
Maslar, Michael. II. Title.
 RC552.B84A88 2009
 616.85'26306--dc22

                                    2009014661

FSC
Mixed Sources
Product group from well-managed forests and other controlled sources
Cert no. SW-COC-002283
www.fsc.org
© 1996 Forest Stewardship Council

11 10 09

10 9 8 7 6 5 4 3 2 1   First printing

To all those in the world whose suffering prevents them from taking part joyously in two of the most simple pleasures, nourishing one's self and being present in one's life.

Contents

Acknowledgments

Regrettably, the list of people who have helped to make this book possible is too long to include in full. However, we would like to acknowledge our spouses and children for kind support, encouragement, understanding, proofreading, patience, and all the rest. We'd also like to thank Marsha Linehan, Shari Manning, Kelly Koerner, Alan Fruzzetti, and all of the other brilliant clinicians and researchers who developed DBT for making this possible in the first place, and for having been such excellent teachers. We're grateful to our consultants on Morita therapy and attention, Mr. James Hill and Mr. Gregg Krech. We also want to thank our clients for having taught us enough to be helpful.

Introduction

If you are reading this, you may suspect that you (or someone you care about) might have an eating disorder. Think about how the following questions may apply:

- Do you ever feel out of control when eating?

- Do you feel guilty, shameful, or sad about your eating habits?

- Do you eat large amounts of food in a short period of time?

- Do you feel the need to exercise, fast, take laxatives, vomit, or use any other behavior to get rid of the calories consumed?

- Do you have trouble coping with strong feelings in general or feelings about your eating or body in particular?

If most of these questions fit you and your experience, you may have bulimia. The good news here is that help is available. It is now known that self-help by itself, or with some assistance, can aid you in overcoming an eating disorder. This book contains the essential information and skills to help you break the cycle of bulimia.

Western society is preoccupied with appearance, and thin is in. Added to this message we constantly hear about the fight against obesity, conveying the message that fat is unacceptable and if you are obese you should fight your body. As a consequence, many women (and increasingly men) in our society have issues with body image and food. At what point are concerns about weight and appearance normal, and when do they become a problem? At what point are people's efforts to control or improve their weight or appearance healthy, and when do those efforts become abnormal? We can all recognize extreme behavior. We identify an eating problem in a person who binges and purges numerous times a day or in one who consumes nothing but lettuce and water. The use of diuretics, laxatives, excessive exercise, or self-induced vomiting to purge food is an easily recognizable symptom of an eating problem.

Likewise, we know that there is an eating disorder in people who are so obese that they can't participate in regular activities and yet continue to consume huge amounts of food. But eating disorders to this degree are the exception, not the norm.

ARE YOUR EATING HABITS A CONCERN?

Because many people have some symptoms of an eating disorder, the question arises: at what point do these symptoms become problematic? The first question to consider is how well you are able to function on a daily basis. For example, are you preoccupied with thoughts of food? Do you often find yourself thinking things like "When will I eat again?"; "What should I eat?"; "Why did I eat that? Why did I eat so much food?"; "How can I keep myself from eating when I am so hungry?"; "How many calories have I eaten today?"; "Was the food at the restaurant prepared with oil, butter, cream, or sugar?"; or "Where can I go to get diet foods?" Do you have constant concerns about body image, constantly fielding thoughts like "I am so fat!"; "I am terrified of being fat"; "How can I lose weight?"; "If I ate that, how much do I have to exercise to burn the calories?"; or "What exercise should I do to get my stomach flat?" Do these concerns make it difficult for you to concentrate and focus on daily activities? Do these concerns make enjoyment difficult? If thoughts of food and body image consume your mind, time, and energy, then you likely have a problem with eating.

Sometimes people don't recognize these symptoms in themselves, but comments from friends and loved ones may call attention to an unrecognized eating problem. For example, do others tell you that you are getting too thin? Do you think that others try to get you to eat more food or to eat more often? Do others comment on how slowly you eat? Do others talk about your great self-control around food? It may be easier for a friend or family member to see these as symptoms of an eating disorder than for you to see the problem. In many ways, these behaviors may work for you. If you are reading this and have concerns about your eating, these worries should be taken seriously. Here are some possible warning signs of developing bulimia nervosa:

- Poor self-esteem

- A sense of self-worth that is increasingly related to weight

- Instability in significant relationships

- Focus on weight and poor body image

- Interest in laxatives, diuretics, exercise, fasting, and occasional bingeing and purging, with the purging being used to manage potential weight gain

As you read this, you may recognize that you're developing some early sign of bulimia nervosa. If that is the case, you should know that the sooner you recognize the problem, the sooner you can get help. The longer eating disorders go untreated, the more resistant they become to treatment.

HELP IS AVAILABLE

If some or many of these signs and symptoms apply to you, the ideas, skills, and exercises in this workbook can be of great help. We have brought together several different approaches to helping people with eating disorders. Each of these approaches has been shown through research to benefit people with bulimia. The first approach addresses motivation, because changing any behavior can be difficult, and changing behaviors related to eating is no different. You may have noticed that some days you feel more strongly that things need to change than other days. You may see how you handle food and your appearance as a problem sometimes, but not at other times. You may be very fed up with your behaviors related to eating or have doubts about your ability to change. As a client once described in an e-mail, "I used [problem eating] behaviors last night, and they spilled onto today. I know I am done with it today, because I want the cycle to end right now and for it not to claim another day. But I'm scared that I don't have what it takes to do it." Feelings of helplessness and confusion around eating disorders are all too common, and that's why we stress motivational therapies in our program and in this book. These techniques will help you build and keep up your desire to change.

But motivation is only one part of change. We recognize that many people need to build a variety of skills in order to change successfully. For example, you may feel very motivated to stop yourself when you are in the middle of a binge, but you may not know how. Or you may find yourself overwhelmed with feeling guilty or sad. These feelings may come along with strong urges to use your eating-disordered behaviors (bingeing, purging, fasting, exercising too much, taking laxatives, and so on). These behaviors typically help to calm or repress these painful feelings. But because of the long-term problems that arise from the use of these disordered behaviors, you will likely eventually want to deal with these feelings in healthier ways. This is where skills and strategies from dialectical behavior therapy (DBT) can give you the tools and strength you need. DBT is a treatment that has been developed to help people who have strong emotions and behaviors that feel out of their control.

The rest of this workbook will take you through a step-by-step approach to understanding and changing the thoughts, feelings, and behaviors you have about food and your appearance that are making you miserable. Each chapter provides new ways of thinking about what is going on for you and exercises that you can use every day to help make your life better. *The Dialectical Behavior Therapy Workbook for Bulimia* can be useful for people as a stand-alone way of helping themselves, but you can also use it as an additional aid if you are already in therapy for bulimia. If you're using this book on your own, remember that some eating problems can be very serious and require the help of an experienced therapist or even an entire program devoted to eating disorders. While we have relied on tested approaches for helping you, we ask that you remain open to seeking out additional help if it seems that your problems are too much for you to handle on your own.

ASSESSING YOUR EATING BEHAVIORS

To begin understanding if your eating habits might be of concern, write down the eating and appearance-focused behaviors, thoughts, and feelings that are problems for you. Then add some detail about why they are so problematic.

_____

_____

_____

_____

_____

_____

Next, write down how you want your life to be. In your ideal life, what would be different about how you relate to food and your appearance? How would your life be different if you were not so consumed by your thoughts of food and body image?

_____

_____

_____

_____

_____

_____

After answering these questions, you can begin to get an idea of whether your life might be more effective, purposeful, and content if you felt less tied into your thoughts, feelings, and behaviors around controlling food in your life. We know it can be scary to face change. But that's why we've provided the information, skills, and encouragement you need to make your life more comfortable and full of joy. Please join us by turning the page now.

CHAPTER 1

What Is Bulimia?

The fact that you've picked up this book likely indicates that you have some idea about what bulimia is. To understand more, let's first look at Annie's experience.

Annie came to us saying that she needed help. Her quality of life was degenerating as everything in her life began taking a backseat to her bulimia. Annie reported that at age fifteen she became aware of her body size and what she was eating because she wanted to be a better athlete. During volleyball practice, the girls were given information packets on how to lose weight, bolstering the idea that Annie's physical being needed work. So she started drinking more water, avoiding desserts, and running more. At this stage, she was able to handle her impulses to shed too many pounds. She lost some weight and felt pretty good about her accomplishment. But as circumstances in her life became more complex and her stress level increased, her handle on body image began to slip. Struggles in school, the tragedy of 9/11, getting her first real boyfriend, and burgeoning symptoms of depression all compounded to increase the pressure she felt to exert control over her weight. Annie found herself purging once after a family meal, but she didn't do it again for a while. Then, with more stress, things got worse with her depression. She was admitted to an adolescent psychiatric unit and was soon transferred to the eating disorders unit as they realized she was making herself vomit up to several times a day. She briefly gained some control over her purging behaviors, but last year she had another slip, and since then the bulimia has spun out of control.

BULIMIA FACTS

Bulimia nervosa is an eating disorder in which a person gets caught in the cycle of bingeing and then "getting rid" of the food. You've had a binge episode if you've eaten a large amount of food (what most people would consider a large amount of food) in a discrete period of time. In addition, while eating you felt out of control. Great feelings of shame can also come while bingeing or after the binge has stopped. If you have bulimia, you have also put forth efforts to compensate or get rid of the food you have binged on. You might have tried purging through vomiting, laxatives, diuretics, or enemas. You might also have compensated by fasting or exercising excessively. People with bulimia also believe the majority of their self-worth is wrapped up in their body image.

As many as one to five out of every hundred women has full-blown bulimia or many of its symptoms (Fitzgibbon, Sánchez-Johnsen, and Martinovich 2003). According to the *Diagnostic and Statistical Manual of Mental Disorders* (American Psychiatric Association 2000), the diagnostic manual used by mental health professionals, it is also known that bulimia occurs in only one-tenth as many men as women.

However, people are only counted if they seek help, and since men are much less likely to seek psychological help than women (especially for an eating disorder, as that is generally viewed as something that only happens to females), this estimate could be low. Because bulimia is more common among women, most of the examples in this book feature women. The incidence of bulimia is similar in most industrialized countries, including the United States, Canada, Australia, and throughout Europe. Bulimia usually starts in the late teen years or early adulthood, and symptoms often begin during or after a period of dieting. Bulimic behaviors may happen relatively consistently or may come and go intermittently. The entire course of bulimia often stretches over several years or more.

THE BULIMIA CYCLE

As you think about bulimia nervosa, it's important that you understand that each of the symptoms interacts with every other symptom. Typically, when you're struggling with bulimia, your weight and body image have a very strong effect on how you feel about yourself. Therefore, if you believe your body isn't perfect, you then decide that you're not a valuable person, and you feel bad about yourself— embarrassed, guilty, angry, sad, and so on. This self-invalidation and negative self-evaluation leads you to feel compelled to change how you look so that you can feel better about yourself. Through the messages of Western culture (for instance, "You're not in the healthy weight range" or "You look different from the women in magazines or on television"), you have learned to invalidate yourself and now believe that losing weight is one powerful way you can feel better.

These thoughts, feelings, and behaviors form a vicious cycle. The cycle begins with you restricting to feel more in control of your weight, which sets you up to binge. Once you've binged, you feel a desperate need to get rid of the calories, so you find a way to do that. You then feel shame for using your eating disorder, and you feel out of control. In order to feel in control again, you decide to restrict—and the cycle continues. For example, you might have begun your attempts at losing weight by trying a diet program (a diet, by definition, encourages caloric restriction). You then noticed that you didn't have the "willpower" to stick to such a restrictive diet. This is a common and culturally supported way to think about dieting. However, rather than being due to a lack of willpower, bingeing often results as a *physiological* response to an overly restrictive diet.

When going without eating for over four hours, your metabolism begins to shut down. This is the point when your body gives up trying to communicate to you that it needs food and the hunger pains stop. Like people, you probably feel better and more in control when the hunger pains temporarily go away. However, you may be thrown for a loop when you realize that the hunger isn't gone for good. Once you allow yourself to eat again, you are much more apt to binge. This reaction is because your hunger becomes so intense that your body wrests control from your mind. Your body *will* be fed, no matter how much control you try to exert. As the definition of a binge indicates, you feel out of control during a binge and ashamed and guilty afterward. This all then leads you back into the cycle of bulimia. This happens because after a binge, you likely try to compensate for the calories consumed. By getting rid of the food through a compensatory behavior like self-induced vomiting, laxative abuse, or compulsive overexercise, you contribute unintentionally to the cycle of bulimia, unintentionally making things worse for yourself.

Once you "empty" your body, you set yourself up for yet another binge. In other words, your body is triggered to binge because it's not getting the calories it needs. Not only does this feed the bulimia, but your embarrassment about the binge might prompt you to start covering up and being dishonest with friends and loved ones to hide what has been going on. These behaviors then lead to even more feelings of shame and guilt, adding fuel to your negative feelings about yourself and pushing you further into the cycle of bulimia. It's important to note that the very behaviors that you have engaged in to make yourself feel better *do* make you feel better in the short run. The problem is that before long, these same behaviors lead to increased emotional pain, loss of control, and even more problem behaviors.

A MODEL FOR UNDERSTANDING BULIMIA

One way to understand bulimia and why it exerts such power in people's lives is to use a model. A *model* in this sense is a psychological term meaning a simplified representation of a more complex process. Models can be straightforward or can include a number of different factors that integrate to form the whole. One integrative model for understanding eating disorders recognizes the biological, psychological, and social components that interact with each other to result in the disorder (the model is *integrative* because it integrates all the elements involved). That is, the way your body works, how you think, and the messages you get from the culture in which you live all combine to make it more or less likely that you will experience bulimia.

The biological component involves factors that can make you vulnerable to eating disorders, including genetics, neurotransmitters in the brain, and other physical traits particular to your individual physiology. Although we know that there is not one specific bulimia gene, studies done on twins show that there are between 50 and 83 percent genetic effects in the heritability of bulimia nervosa (Bulik, Sullivan, and Kendler 1998). Heritability estimates reflect the amount of variation in genetic effects compared to the amount of variation in environmental effects. So we know that genetics plays a significant role in determining who develops bulimia.

The psychological and social components of bulimia include high *comorbidity rates*, meaning that bulimia often is seen in people who also suffer from anxiety, depression, substance abuse, post-traumatic stress disorder, or obsessive-compulsive disorder. If you are struggling with bulimia, then you probably also have trouble regulating your emotions, and one disorder often makes the other worse. For example, when the symptoms of your depression crop up, that sadness and lack of energy can make it more likely that you'll engage in bulimic behaviors. The psychological and social components of bulimia also involve how you interact with family, friends, and Western culture in general and how those interactions affect how you think and feel. For instance, you may receive messages from those around you and from the culture at large that lead you to believe that body weight is of primary importance. You might receive messages indicating that being thin is powerful and not being thin means you're weak. Or because of social and cultural messages, you may believe that those who are thin are loved, admired, and appreciated, while those who are fat are disgusting and unlovable. The interaction between invalidating messages from family, friends, and society and the biological factors mentioned above leads to and perpetuates the cycle of bulimia. Furthermore, the bulimic behaviors themselves (restrictive eating, excessive exercising, bingeing and purging) alter your body and brain chemistry and can impair your ability to think clearly. This impairment can increase your difficulty with self-control and make the whole situation worse.

UNDERSTANDING WHAT BULIMIA DOES FOR YOU

Most people tend to focus on all the reasons their bulimia is so "bad." It is just as important to understand how and why it has been helpful. Clearly, there *are* benefits to having bulimia—if there weren't, you would have no problem stopping the behaviors. While we can definitely acknowledge that bulimia is dangerous and damaging to the body and mind, you do it because it helps you cope. For example, when Cara was overwhelmed with the pressures of work, she found herself turning to food. This choice helped her cope because she was able to focus on the food instead of her stressors. As she ate, she forgot about her work anxiety, and when she was done purging she was exhausted and fell asleep. Now consider the benefits you experience from your bulimia.

What You Gain from Bulimia

This exercise will help you examine the benefits that you feel from turning to your eating disorder by looking at your feelings before and after a binge. Then you will compare those feelings to how you *think* you feel before and after a binge. It's important that you do this investigation when you aren't feeling vulnerable to a binge, so you can discern your feelings more accurately. You will be remembering how you usually feel before and after bingeing and purging and then writing down your feelings right after bingeing and purging. This comparison will show you the benefits you gain from your bulimia. You will also see that what you gain from using your eating disorder is temporary, while the harm is more long-term.

Write down how you typically feel before a binge and rate those feelings on a scale of 1 to 10 (with 1 being least intense feeling and 10 being most intense feeling ever). List emotions that you feel and thoughts that commonly run through your head at these times. Complete the first step when you are calm, able to think clearly, and without bulimic behaviors (that is, not just before a binge). Then, when you're feeling like you might start or have just started a binge, write down how you feel at that moment.

What you recall typically feeling before a binge and what you recall as the intensity of those feelings on a scale of 1 to 10:

_____

_____

| 1 | 2 | 3 | 4 | 5 | 6 | 7 | 8 | 9 | 10 |

What you actually feel right before a binge and the intensity of those feelings on a scale of 1 to 10:

_____

_____

| 1 | 2 | 3 | 4 | 5 | 6 | 7 | 8 | 9 | 10 |

Next, write down how you typically feel after a purge. First, do this at a time when you are calm, able to think clearly, and without purging behaviors (not just after purging). Then, right after a time when you have purged, write down how you are feeling right at that moment.

What you recall typically feeling after purging, and what you recall as the intensity of those feelings on a scale of 1 to 10:

_____

_____

| 1 | 2 | 3 | 4 | 5 | 6 | 7 | 8 | 9 | 10 |

What you actually feel right after a binge/purge episode and the intensity of those feelings on a scale of 1 to 10:

_____

_____

| 1 | 2 | 3 | 4 | 5 | 6 | 7 | 8 | 9 | 10 |

If you said that after a binge/purge episode you felt calmer or went to sleep, then you already understand how bulimic behaviors can help you to feel better and regulate emotion in the moment. In a similar way, you will likely notice that you rated the intensity of your feelings much lower when you were calmer and not actually bingeing or purging, and your feelings were likely more intense immediately before and after the bingeing and purging. Our client Annie wrote about this in an e-mail:

> I know you've noticed that I have been very calm during our last couple of sessions. I believe I was calm because, right before the last couple sessions, I binged/purged. I usually feel very calm after I do this. The e-mails I've sent you are usually during a no-binge time, and that's why I sound so much more upset in the e-mails than when I've been in session with you. I am so much more depressed and anxious right before a binge or when I'm not using behaviors.

So Annie used bulimia as a way to calm her feelings and cope, and it often worked pretty effectively for her in this regard. But bulimia is not a viable long-term option. While these behaviors can help you to cope in the moment, they make things much worse in the long run by leading you into a repetitious cycle of painful feelings, harmful physical repercussions, and ultimately a sense of being out of control and needing to escape. And the more you use bulimic behaviors to escape from your painful feelings, the more those feelings rear their ugly heads, leading you into a vicious cycle.

CONCLUSION

There are effective treatments to help you step out of this cycle, which is why we wrote this book. Although we must recognize that there are benefits to your bulimia, we remind you that those benefits are greatly outweighed by the damaging effects of the behaviors. As you continue to read, you'll learn more effective and sustainable ways to cope with uncomfortable feelings, to again take pleasure in the human joy of nourishing yourself, and to gain some true control over your life.

CHAPTER 2

What Is Dialectical Behavior Therapy?

Dialectical behavior therapy, or DBT, is a helping approach developed by Marsha Linehan, Ph.D. (1993a), and many others. Originally designed for people who had repeated suicide attempts, it evolved into a treatment for a specific kind of personality disorder and more recently has been researched and used as a therapy for people with other complicated and persistent problems. Recent clinical studies have shown support for DBT as helpful to people with bulimia (Safer, Telch, and Agras 2001; Telch, Agras, and Linehan 2001).

HOW DBT WORKS

DBT works by helping people gain a very clear and detailed understanding of their problems and what they can do in step-by-step fashion to change them. More specifically, DBT can help you identify what particular behaviors cause problems, exactly what types of situations, thoughts, feelings, and other behaviors lead to these problems, and what new behaviors or skills you can use to prevent the problem behaviors from occurring. These strategies, first introduced by Marsha Linehan (1993a), are called *chain analysis* (figuring out what happened) and *solution analysis* (figuring out how to change it).

For example, applying DBT strategies, Katie figured out the progression of thoughts, feelings, and behaviors in her binges. By using a chain analysis of one episode of bingeing, she learned that one situation prompting her problem behavior was being home alone at night with no plan for how to spend her time. She figured out that, after getting out of her work clothes and eating a very small dinner, she sat down and stopped all her activity. She looked around her empty apartment and began to feel lonely. Her feelings of loneliness led to thoughts about her appearance, such as "People really don't like to be around me because I'm so fat." She then started to feel ashamed and irritated with herself, leading to more self-critical thoughts like "I'm just a loser." She cycled through these thoughts and others like them for a while, feeling worse and worse. Meanwhile, her hunger mounted. As her feelings increased, she experienced a greater and greater sense of being out of control. She then found herself pacing from room to room, eventually ending up in the kitchen. At this point, the sight of the crackers on her countertop got her eating. When she started eating, her attention was then drawn away from her feelings, and she felt relief. Unfortunately, she ate the entire box of crackers, all of the cream cheese in the refrigerator, and then all of the ice cream in the freezer. By the time she had finished, she noticed that she felt full, but she also felt very embarrassed and angry with herself. The feelings of fullness, embarrassment, and anger quickly led again to a sense of being out of control. Unable to tolerate these experiences, Katie quickly went to the bathroom. Tears welling in her eyes, she purged. When she finished, she sat back on her heels on the bathroom floor feeling tired and numb. The unbearable feelings were gone now, but only for a time. As thoughts about what she did came back to her later, the embarrassment, anger, and sense of being out of control returned. She realized that this set the stage for everything to happen all over again.

When Katie thought about how all this happened, she realized that bingeing functioned to help her manage painful feelings—she had relief when she started to eat. Yet the binge itself led to more emotional pain. Looking further at the chain of events, she saw that purging also helped her to manage feelings. Purging helped her feel numb rather than in miserable. Unfortunately, not long afterward, she felt painful emotions again. Her behaviors helped her in the moment, but they also put her right back into the cycle.

After identifying this pattern, Katie then figured out how to substitute new behaviors and skills to change the triggering situation and manage the thoughts and feelings that built up to the binge. She decided that having a plan for at least some of her time each evening after work was very helpful for her. She also determined that eating only a small dinner left her vulnerable to increased hunger before the end of the evening. She made a commitment to use DBT skills to help. She used emotion regulation skills to help ease her feelings of loneliness, embarrassment, and anger. She practiced mindfulness skills that helped her stay focused on the present rather then on regrets about the past or fears about the future. Finally, for situations when these strategies weren't enough, she developed a crisis plan of several distress tolerance skills for use when feeling extremely agitated. You will learn how to use each of these sets of skills (mindfulness, emotion regulation, distress tolerance, and others) later in this book.

Katie's story shows how DBT can help you change your behavior in order to solve problems. DBT assumes that most problem behaviors actually function to solve some other problem that you have. In Katie's example, her bingeing helped her to solve the problem of having intense and painful emotions; when she started to binge, she immediately got distracted from her emotions and felt relief. The important thing to keep in mind here is that bingeing and other problem behaviors only solve problems in the short run, tending to make things worse in the long run. Bingeing did help Katie to stop feeling bad during the time she was bingeing. Not too long afterward, however, the binge led her to feel embarrassed and angry again anyway, and the behavior didn't help her solve the problems that led her to feel that way in the first place. One of the major goals of DBT is to help you find effective, nondamaging ways to solve problems, methods that can have longer-term benefits. As Katie became more skillful in handling her feelings, she felt more in control of her life. As she felt more in control, she found that she criticized herself less. While changing was very hard for Katie in the beginning, as she practiced new behaviors and experienced more desirable results, it got easier for her to use healthier ways to behave and cope.

Your Chain Analysis

Now it's time for you to give chain analysis a try. Take this opportunity to figure out what triggered your last episode of bingeing and purging. Think back to the last time you binged and purged and try to remember what actually happened. You may not recall all of the details—that's understandable. Just do your best. As you work with chain analysis, you'll get better and better at remembering the details of incidents. For now, just do your best answering the questions below.

What was the prompting event? What happened in your environment? What did you become aware of? Who said what to whom? What changes occurred around you that set you on a path toward your last binge/purge episode?

_____

_____

What was your immediate reaction to the prompting event above? What did you think? What did you feel? What did you do?

_____

_____

What other links in the chain happened between the prompting event and your binge/purge episode? What other things did you think, feel, or do? What other events occurred?

_____

_____

What happened immediately before the binge/purge episode? If you had a thought that you were going to start eating, what happened just before the thought? If you found yourself just heading to the kitchen, as an example, what happened right before you started to move? What did you think, feel (very important), or do (also very important)?

_____

_____

As you binged, how did you feel?

_____

_____

As you binged, what thoughts did you have?

_____

_____

Immediately after your binge, how did you feel?

_____

_____

Immediately after your binge, what thoughts did you have?

_____

_____

How did you feel later, maybe half an hour or more after the binge?

_____

_____

What thoughts did you have later, maybe half an hour or more after the binge?

_____

_____

As you purged, how did you feel?

_____

_____

As you purged, what thoughts did you have?

_____

_____

Immediately after your purge, how did you feel?

_____

_____

Immediately after your purge, what thoughts did you have?

_____

_____

How did you feel later, maybe half an hour or more after the purge?

_____

_____

What thoughts did you have later, maybe half an hour or more after the purge?

_____

_____

As you look back over the chain analysis, can you think of anything you could have done differently to break the chain leading to bingeing and purging? (Don't worry if you can't think of anything right now. We will spend a lot of time on this topic in later chapters as we discuss DBT skills.)

_____

_____

WHY IS IT CALLED DIALECTICAL BEHAVIOR THERAPY?

So far, we've looked at the behavior part of DBT. As you can tell, we've been examining how DBT can help you understand behavior so that you can change it. An important thing that the creators of DBT learned, however, is that working to change complicated and persistent problems is usually only part of the solution. Most people with problems that are involved and chronic (including bulimia) find themselves swinging painfully back and forth between many extremes: first restricting or purging, then bingeing. You may be completely sure you have a serious problem in one moment and later conclude that things are really okay. You probably sometimes feel thoroughly overwhelmed by painful emotions, only to feel numb or empty later.

In order to help people deal with these painful and confusing extremes, Marsha Linehan and her colleagues incorporated the philosophy of *dialectics* (1993a). The theory of dialectics concludes that we see things in the world and take action in terms of opposites. As we grow and develop, however, we often work to bring together things that we see as opposite and incompatible, combining them into more inclusive and useful wholes. For example, as a young child you might have learned that going near fire was bad and staying away from it was good. This was useful at the time, because without the proper understanding and skills, you could have hurt yourself and others by using fire. As you grew up, you probably learned that going near fire was no longer bad, and staying away was no longer good. For instance, you had to go near fire to cook. Using fire was no longer just bad or just good—it depended how you used it.

Similarly, you may find yourself thinking about food as the source of feeling bad about yourself and want as little to do with it as possible. But at other times it seems clear that you need food to feel better. So, does food make you feel good or bad? The answer is both, depending upon how you use it. Part of the recovery from bulimia involves seeing and using food in a *balanced* way so that it is neither something that is bad for you nor something that you must use in unhealthy ways in order to feel better.

AN IMPORTANT DIALECTIC: ACCEPTANCE AND CHANGE

One of the most important dialectics to understand and act on in DBT is the dialectic of *acceptance and change*. To most people, these two terms seem incompatible: "I can't accept myself as I am. I have so many problems! If I accept myself, then I'll *never* change."

Here's a dialectical way of looking at change and acceptance: "In order to change how I am, I have to accept the way I really am first. In order to really accept myself, I have to change the way I think about and act toward myself." In this way of thinking, change cannot happen without acceptance, and acceptance cannot happen without change.

Returning to Katie's example, if she didn't accept that having a small dinner (restricting) really set her up for intense hunger later, she couldn't change in a way that was helpful to her by eating reasonable portions.

Acceptance is a very complicated topic, but it's also crucial to success. That's why we're broaching the subject early in the book—to lay a foundation for understanding. However, though acceptance can be challenging to some, DBT has several skills to help you move toward accepting. We'll be exploring these skills and helpful ways to think about acceptance as we move through the book. For now, try the exercise below to begin grasping how you consider acceptance and change.

Accepting or Rejecting New Ideas

To help you get started understanding and working on acceptance, it will be helpful to take some time to identify some of your thoughts, feelings, and behaviors related to bulimia. Here we'll be looking at things you may have difficulty accepting or wish you could deny.

Look at the chain analysis you did earlier. Then think about some of the information we've presented so far. Have you found yourself rejecting anything or wishing something was not the way it is? List what you find yourself rejecting. See if you can then open yourself to thinking more about what you have rejected as you read further in the book.

_____

_____

_____

_____

_____

_____

CONCLUSION

In this chapter, we introduced dialectical behavior therapy, or DBT. We discussed how the DBT strategy of chain analysis is used to understand problem behaviors and how solution analysis is applied to help figure out how to use DBT skills to change those problem behaviors. We then walked you through the steps of doing a chain analysis on your bulimic behavior. You then learned about dialectics and how using them can help you understand the swings you probably experience between different extremes of behavior and emotion. We then discussed the important dialectic of acceptance and change, and you started to work on acceptance by identifying ideas we have gone over so far that you reject. In the next chapter, we'll go over strategies to help you maintain and increase your motivation to change by helping you figure out and act on your purpose.

CHAPTER 3

Following Your Purpose

Now that you have some understanding of what bulimia is and how DBT works, the next big question is "How do I get myself to do what it takes?" To begin, you need to find a purpose for your motivation. People often say things like "I can't make changes unless I find the motivation"; "I need to feel motivated"; or "I need to figure out why I'm not motivated." The problem with this approach is that it usually proves ineffective at actually motivating change consistently and in a reasonable amount of time. Reading this chapter and completing the exercises will help you build valuable skills toward staying committed and motivated. First let's look at your readiness for change.

STAGES OF CHANGE

Before you can really commit to change you must have an idea of how ready you really are to change. There are five stages of change that have been conceptualized for a variety of problem behaviors (Prochaska and DiClemente 1983). The five stages are precontemplation, contemplation, preparation, action, and maintenance. *Precontemplation* is the stage in which there is no intention to change your behaviors because they work for you or because you're not even aware that you have a problem. Since you have picked up this workbook, we can assume you are at least in the stage of contemplating change. In the stage of *contemplation*, you are aware that a problem exists, in this case with bulimia, and you are seriously thinking about working on and committing to overcoming it, but you haven't yet made the commitment to take the necessary action. In the stage of *preparation*, you are likely planning on taking action in the near future, but you have not effectively taken action up to this point. In the *action* stage you do what you need to do to create a life worth being present in. Action involves behavioral changes, and taking action requires a considerable commitment of time and energy. Finally, the stage of *maintenance* is when you work to prevent relapse and strengthen the gains you've made during the action stage.

Assessing Your Stage of Change

Before moving on in the workbook it's important that you understand where you are in the stages of change. So answer the following questions to see where you're at right now.

Do you think you have a problem with bulimia? _____

Do you have the desire to stop using bulimic behaviors? _____

Are you seriously thinking about working on and committing to overcoming the bulimia? _____

Are you planning on taking action in the near future? Did you buy this workbook to take action toward recovery?

_____

Are you currently doing all that you can do to recover? _____

Are you eating healthfully? Do you need to see a nutritionist? Do you need to join a skills training group? Have you committed the time and energy to create a life worth being present in?

_____

_____

_____

What are you doing to prevent relapse? Are you practicing any behavioral change skills regularly?

_____

   After filling out the answers to these questions, you can better assess how you're feeling about change. Keep in mind that you can return to this section of the workbook anytime you need to reassess your stage of change. It can help you become more aware of where you are and what you might need to do to move through the stages.

IDENTIFYING YOUR PURPOSE

As you move through the stages of contemplation, preparation, and action, it will help to have a sense of purpose for this significant change. When getting motivated and staying motivated, it's important that you learn to identify your own personal purpose. Your *purpose* is what you are working toward experiencing. Any given person has a multitude of purposes in life at any given time. A purpose can be as complex as recovery or as simple as doing the dishes for the maintenance of your living space. Since you have picked up this book, we assume that one of the purposes you are considering is to live a life without an eating disorder. It can be helpful to first begin looking at what the pros and cons might be of having your eating disorder. To really recover you must understand what bulimia does for you (both helpful and hurtful). To gain a more nuanced view of your eating disorder and what it does to help and harm you, fill out the pros and cons chart below.

The Pros and Cons of Bulimia

Pros of Using Bulimia	Cons of Using Bulimia
For example: I don't feel my painful emotions when using behaviors.	For example: I lie to my friends so I don't have to go out to eat with them.

Pros of Not Using Bulimia	Cons of Not Using Bulimia
For example: I feel more productive and present.	For example: I have to feel my painful emotions.

As you can see, having an eating disorder helps you and it hurts you. So if it helps, why stop using it? Why recover? Why use this book? To answer these questions, you need to use the pros and cons information as you again think about formulating a healthy purpose. This pros and cons exercise can also be very helpful as you work through the stages of contemplation and preparation in helping you realize that the pros of using your bulimia (escape feelings, avoidance, numbness, and so on) are usually short-term gains, while the cons are longer-term (health consequences, relationship consequences, shame, and so on). Likewise, the pros of not using your bulimia (being more present in life and in relationships) are long-term, while the cons are short-lived (having to tolerate the feeling that you want to escape).

In this book, finding your purpose means figuring out what you are working toward. What are your healthy-minded goals? By picking up this book, you have taken one step toward a healthy purpose. After filling out the pros and cons chart you can see that some of the greatest benefits from your bulimia are that you check out, disconnect from feelings, and stop thinking about your problems and stressors temporarily. DBT was originally created to help people develop a life worth fully living, because the population that it was created for often feels that life isn't worth the effort (Linehan 1993b). With bulimia, this purpose can be a bit modified. Because bulimia is most often used as a method of checking out or disconnecting from one's emotional dysregulation, the purpose when using DBT is to create a life worth being present in. Now that you are choosing this purpose, you might be wondering how you can maintain the purpose and stay committed to it. Keep reading.

MOTIVATION AND MORITA THERAPY

To begin to answer the question of how to maintain your purpose and stay committed, let's take a look at a very old type of Japanese psychology called *Morita therapy* (Morita et al. 1998). Morita therapy was developed in the early part of the twentieth century by a Japanese psychiatrist named Shoma Morita. Morita was influenced by the psychological principles of Zen Buddhism, placing the general concept of acceptance at the base of his therapy. Morita recognized that feelings are natural responses to life circumstances. He taught that you should accept your internal experience without question, and that attention to your internal experience is what actually causes suffering. For the purposes of this workbook, we've modified this idea to focus on acceptance of thoughts, feelings, and bodily sensations that aren't within your control. Morita realized that, instead of trying to change thoughts and feelings or get rid of them, one needs to accept them and learn to coexist with them. In other words, you need to accept your automatic thoughts (thoughts that just pop into your head) and feelings as not within your control and then act for a purpose, regardless. Remember, at this point the purpose is to create a life worth being present in. Can you have thoughts that are contrary to your purpose and do what is important to you anyway? Can you think one way and choose to behave another? This idea may seem a bit foreign to you because, like most of us, you are often being driven by your thoughts or emotions. Think about the last time you had planned on doing something but then, at the last minute, you changed your mind because you lost your motivation, sight of your purpose, or willingness to do what you had committed to. It's important to be aware of how often you acknowledge that some action is likely a healthy idea, yet you don't act on it and aren't even sure why. If you can become aware of these times, then you can learn to use skills to stay on task and focused on your healthy purpose, improving your motivation and returning to your willingness to do whatever it takes to stay committed and follow through with the necessary actions.

For example, before Cara could begin to eat healthfully, she had to go grocery shopping. In the overall purpose of recovery, one goal for her was to go grocery shopping regularly and efficiently. Yet every time she tried to go, she became very anxious, and she ended up bingeing and purging on junk food from a vending machine. The grocery store experience was so overwhelming to her that she had to find a way to cope, and her coping mechanism of bingeing was not a healthy option. Once Cara became aware of her anxiety and how this strong feeling contributed to her decrease in motivation, she was able to problem solve. She asked a friend to accompany her to the store for support, and she began shopping at night when the stores were much less crowded. She was able to follow through with her goal of going to the grocery store because she was focused on the need to act on her commitment to her purpose of recovery.

See the table below to understand the need to act for your purpose.

Modified Morita Table

Uncontrollable	Controllable
Automatic thoughts Feelings Sensations	Conscious or Deliberate thoughts Actions
Accept your automatic thoughts, feelings, and sensations as they are and accept that they aren't within your control.	Act for your purpose. This needs to be a healthy purpose that you commit to.

When looking for motivation, most people like to wait for their thoughts, feelings, or bodily sensations to tell them when they are motivated. In fact, people spend a lot of time in therapy trying to understand why they do or do not do something. However, the truth about finding motivation is that waiting for thoughts, feelings, and sensations to help you become motivated for change is not always going to work. Feelings and sensations are not within your control, thoughts only sometimes are, and none of them are constant. If you wait for your automatic thoughts, feelings, or sensations to motivate action, then you have no idea how long it will take to become motivated. Your motivation will ebb and flow with your moods. One day you might be really motivated, and the next day you're not. However, if you can accept that you can't control feelings, sensations, and automatic thoughts, and therefore you can't use them to motivate action, you can find motivation in your ultimate purpose. Purpose is constant, and you can control it—you can make a choice! When you have automatic thoughts, feelings, and sensations that tell you to ignore your purpose, you can just bring those thoughts, feelings, and sensations along with you as you continue to act for your purpose.

To illustrate how this plays out, here is a simple example that you might identify with. Emily is a therapist working in a major metropolitan area. She wakes up at 5:30 AM on Tuesdays and Thursdays because she begins seeing clients at 7:00 AM. When her alarm goes off at 5:30, all her thoughts, feelings, and bodily sensations scream, "Stay in bed!" But still she gets up. Why and how can she haul herself out of bed when she wants so desperately to go back to sleep? She has a purpose. She has a purpose to be there for her clients to help them. She has a purpose to her career (she might get fired if she doesn't show up). She has a purpose to help financially support her family. She notices her automatic thoughts, feelings, and bodily sensations, and she takes them with her as she acts for her purpose. She notices them and doesn't discount them—but she still acts for the purpose that she's committed to.

Now, you might ask, "What if one day my purpose is to be healthy, and the next day I think my purpose is to be the thinnest person in the room?" The answer lies in the key word "think." If you *think* your purpose has changed, you can notice those automatic thoughts and take them with you as you continue to act for your true purpose. You have committed to working on having a life worth being present in. Remember, your purpose is one you have decided upon and committed to in a healthy state of mind. You can't pretend that those competing thoughts don't exist, and you need to recognize them. At the same time, you don't need to *act* on those competing thoughts because you are acting for your purpose. When you suddenly think you have a change in purpose, look at what has changed in your environment or your life that could lead to a change in purpose. In an e-mail, Gregg Krech (an author and expert on Japanese approaches to mental health) explained, "When we are considering abandoning one purpose for another and there is no external change in circumstances, it often means that the shift in purpose is simply a shift in our thoughts or feelings. So we can ask the question 'What has changed?' as a way of testing the value of abandoning a purpose that we had committed to." If you've asked yourself "What has changed?" and nothing really has, then you can also try to become aware, to notice, or to be mindful of what wants to change your purpose. Where do those thoughts come from?

THE CONCEPT OF ED MIND

To understand more clearly what we mean by "What wants to change your purpose?" let us first explain the concept of your eating disorder as a state of mind. Sure, it's a collection of thoughts, feeling, and behaviors. But for right now, let's consider it a state of mind.

A good way of understanding this state of mind is to think of your eating disorder as an internal abusive spouse. This concept is introduced in *Life Without Ed* (2004), a book by Jenni Schafer and Thom Rutledge in which the authors personify this abusive state of mind as a spouse named Ed. (Ed stands for eating disorder.) The idea is that the more you listen to this state of mind, this "abusive spouse," the more you get trapped in the abusive cycle. The *Ed mind* is an internal state of mind that's hypercritical and abusively judgmental. It's important to understand the parallels between the control exerted by this internal critical voice and the control exerted by an abusive partner.

Your Ed thoughts act like an internal abusive spouse. The similarities include issues of isolation, seduction, and the ensuing cycle of abuse and praise. An abusive spouse will first seduce you with promises of making your life better while helping you handle your stress by making you feel good—for the time being. It's easy to miss the fact that an abusive spouse wants to control you so that you do whatever he wants. As one aspect of this control, he keeps you from fulfilling your dreams and aspirations and gets you to trade them for what he wants. He will lie to you, manipulate you, and control you. In the case of bulimia, Ed mind takes control of you with the only concern being to get you to be the thinnest person you can possibly be.

Ed mind also first gets your attention or seduces you by helping you deal with stress by giving you something else to focus all of your attention on. Ed mind tells you that Ed will solve your problems and take care of you. You can focus on food to eat or not eat, when you will eat, how you'll get rid of the calories, how you'll keep yourself from eating, and so on, instead of thinking about the things that are stressful in your life.

Like an abusive spouse who isolates his victim by telling her that no one else cares about her like he does, Ed will slowly isolate you by telling you that others don't care about you or aren't thinking about your best interests like he is. He will tell you that they lie to you because they're jealous, or that they're the ones who want to control you. The abusive spouse wants to keep you as far away from those who love you as he possibly can.

Once you are isolated and without support, the abusive spouse will begin the cycle of abuse. After an episode of abuse, you are promised that things won't get that bad again. But the abuse *does* begin again. This cycle repeats and repeats, and you begin to feel unable to escape. You are told that you're safe when you obey and that you're pathetic and stupid if you don't.

Your Abusive Ed Mind

Now let's look at how your Ed mind has been abusive. Give the following questions some long thought and answer them to the best of your ability.

What was going on in your life when you first began to use your eating disorder? What stressors did you have, what losses did you experience? What did Ed come to rescue you from?

_____

_____

_____

How did Ed help you? Did he help you check out? Did he help you focus on food and body image so that you didn't have to think about other disturbing things?

_____

_____

How did Ed isolate you? Did you socialize less so that you didn't have to deal with food? Did you often cancel on friends because you were upset about how you looked and didn't want to be seen? Do you lie to those who care because you're trying to protect Ed?

_____

_____

_____

What are your Ed thoughts that push others away? Does Ed tell you that no one cares? Does Ed tell you that people just want you to be fat when they express concern about your eating patterns? Does Ed tell you that you are too fat to be cared about?

_____

_____

_____

What does the cycle of abuse look like? Does Ed tell you that you're wonderful and strong one minute and then fat and pathetic the next? Does Ed tell you to not eat all day and then tell you to eat everything in sight?

_____

_____

_____

As you are likely noticing, Ed mind is a state that includes thoughts like "You are so selfish and pathetic"; "When you eat you're being self-indulgent"; "Everyone just wants you to get fat, and you can only trust Ed"; and "If you use Ed behaviors, you'll feel better and your problems will be under control." These thoughts, and the trap of believing these thoughts, are driven by strong emotions such as shame, guilt, and rage. The only goals that Ed mind has are for you to be to be the thinnest person at any cost and to check out from your present life as much as possible so that you're solely focused on Ed. Now that you can more clearly see the abusive cycle, it will be helpful if you can remember this when Ed offers his false promises that things will only get better with him.

STICKING TO YOUR PURPOSE IN SPITE OF ED MIND

Now that you understand Ed mind, what motivates Ed mind, and how Ed mind functions, how do you continue acting for a purpose when Ed mind can be so loud and persistent? First, you need to make sure that it's a healthy purpose and that you aren't acting for a purpose generated from Ed mind. Ed mind will likely tell you not to read this because he thinks this sounds like hooey, but that is again how Ed mind controls you. If you take a chance and read this, the skills might actually help, and then Ed mind becomes less powerful. Ed mind will tell you any lies to get you to put this workbook down so that you don't begin the process of change. Ed mind might tell you that it will take too much work or effort, that it sounds too difficult, or that it won't help anyway. Regardless of what Ed mind says, you can decide to notice those thoughts generated from Ed mind and act for your purpose by continuing to work with this book. The following is an example of how Annie used her Morita purpose to help her with Ed mind:

> I've been doing well this week, despite Ed whispering in my ear. He has been wanting me to steal money or steal the keys from my mom while she's sleeping. He wants me to steal change

from the community jar to go to the Dollar Tree to buy really cheap binge food. Ed wants me to order another credit card (I cut up my other one) and use it for binge food. I have been combating it with my new purpose (my purpose is to be healthy), and that seems to help. After I say that to myself, I usually go find something to do like clean, read, play with my cat, or homework.

Jenni Schafer and Thom Rutledge suggest that when learning to separate yourself from Ed mind, it can be helpful to begin writing dialogues between your healthy self and your Ed mind (2004). As an example of this dialoguing skill, look at Margaret's dialogue.

Ed: Oh my God! Look at what your mom brought home for dinner—fat in a cardboard box. You cannot eat that. Oh, don't tell me you're thinking about it, Margaret!

Margaret: Cheese pizza is what's for dinner. I haven't had that in ages. I remember it being decent. I think I may have enjoyed it once. Oh, and look—crazy bread. I know I love crazy bread.

Ed: Margaret, do you love being fat? Because that is what you will be if you eat that.

Margaret: A piece of cheese pizza and two crazy bread sticks aren't going to make me fat, Ed. The binges you tell me to go on will, though. Those don't help me deal with problems. But I have a feeling that if I eat this pizza you'll shut up, and even if you don't, I have a feeling I'll feel better about me if I don't give into you.

Ed: Fat in a box! This is ridiculous. Where is the control? Margaret, this is insane! Boy, how the mighty have fallen. I thought you were something… I thought we were a team. You aren't playing your part. I can't keep you skinny with no effort from you. I'd need a steel muzzle to keep food out of your trap!

Margaret: Who says I can't be skinny and eat a piece of pizza and some crazy bread, Ed? You aren't making sense again. I'm going upstairs to eat dinner.

Ed: Okay, but if you eat that tonight, no food later or tomorrow! And when your girlfriends ask you why you aren't eating, just make up a lie about how your parents wanted to go out for a late breakfast and you ate quite a bit because you were feeling that you could finally say no to me and order the breakfast of pancakes you've been wanting to order. That sounds good. It sounds like you. Maybe add "a breakfast the size of Canada" to that for authenticity. Now it really sounds like you. Good. We'll go with that.

Margaret: We're not going anywhere, unless you're eating pizza too. Oh, and later, if I'm hungry, I'm going to eat. I'm eating breakfast tomorrow, and I'm eating lunch with friends. I could not skip out on dinner, either.

Ed: Well, good-bye skinny, hello cow.

Margaret: Yup, Ed. You say what you want. I know I'm not a cow.

As you read through this dialogue, you can see how relentless, manipulative, and convincing the Ed-mind voice can be. People often say that they don't even notice a difference between themselves and Ed mind because they've become so fused with the Ed way of thinking. It's imperative that you begin to learn to separate so that you can use your DBT skills when Ed mind is causing self-destructive behaviors.

Separating from Ed Mind

To help you begin to notice and separate from the internally abusive, hypercritical thoughts of Ed mind, try this exercise. Next time you use your bulimic behaviors (next time you binge, purge, overexercise, and so on) write down your thoughts below. If there is any part of you that doesn't want to engage in behaviors, list them as healthy thoughts. List the parts of you that do want to use behaviors as Ed-mind thoughts. You can write down the dialogue that usually goes on in your head when you struggle with these behaviors. When you notice an Ed-mind thought, write it down and then come up with a healthy counter thought in response to the Ed thought. Write a dialogue as Margaret did, above.

Ed-mind thoughts: _____

_____

Healthy thoughts: _____

_____

Ed-mind thoughts: _____

_____

Healthy thoughts: _____

_____

Ed-mind thoughts: _____

_____

Healthy thoughts: _____

_____

Ed-mind thoughts: _____

_____

Healthy thoughts: _____

_____

Sometimes Ed mind will make a lot of sense to you, and sometimes you'll be able to see the lies and deceit. Either way, it's important that you keep trying to distinguish your healthy voice from Ed mind.

After reading about Margaret's experience, and after beginning the separation from Ed mind, you can see that when the healthy voice tries to take a stand, Ed mind takes the information and tries to use it against the healthy voice. You can also see how futile it can be to try to argue with Ed mind using logic, because Ed mind does not use logic. Ed lives in emotion mind. When discussing mindfulness (which we'll be exploring more in chapter 5), Marsha Linehan described three mind states—emotion mind, rational mind, and wise mind (1993a). *Emotion mind* is a state of mind in which you function from raw emotions. Urges are experienced from strong emotions, action is taken from strong emotions, and it is much more likely that your purpose becomes checking out from strong emotions instead of creating a life worth being present in. We'll be examining emotion mind in much greater detail in chapters 5 and 6. What should be clear at this point is that Ed mind is abusive and relentless, and it will not ease up or go away. If you don't become aware of and choose not to give in to Ed mind, your life will be run by Ed. With this understanding, as you approach the issue of motivation, just ask yourself if you *really* want to spend the rest of your life engaging with Ed mind so that everything else important in your life becomes secondary. If you don't continually work toward a life worth being present in, then you will check out, likely creating more problems for yourself and leading to even more stress and problems that you want to check out from.

MORE HELP WITH MOTIVATION: NAIKAN

To help you focus on your healthy-minded purpose instead of your Ed-minded purpose, you can look at another type of Eastern philosophy: Naikan. *Naikan* is a Japanese word that means "introspection." This philosophy, developed in the 1940s by a devout Buddhist named Ishin Yashimoto, is a structured method of self-reflection that can help you to look at yourself, your relationships, and your actions from a new perspective.

This philosophy is discussed in depth in the book *Naikan: Gratitude, Grace, and the Japanese Art of Self-Reflection*, by Greg Krech (2002). To read more about Naikan reflections and see more examples, go to www.todoinstitute.org. Naikan involves the use of an ongoing self-reflective exercise. When examining any relationship, ask yourself:

- What have I received?

- What have I given?

- What difficulty have I caused?

Traditionally these questions are used to examine the most important relationships of our lives. Since you struggle with bulimia, it is clear that your relationship to your eating disorder is one of the most primary relationships in your life. Therefore, the Naikan questions can be posed in relationship to Ed mind:

- What have I received from Ed?

  The beneficial aspects of comfort, avoidance, attention, and so on

- What have I given to Ed?

  Money, time, health, attention, potential

- What difficulties have I caused others due to my relationship with Ed?

  Concern, money, time, distraction

Understanding Your Relationship with Ed

As you go through this exercise you'll see that you have given plenty to Ed and Ed has also given to you. While you may have considered how Ed has impacted your life and the lives of those you love, Ed has likely gotten you to feel so bad about it that you used behaviors to avoid thinking about it or feeling that pain. By doing this exercise you can see the facts more objectively. This exercise is about acknowledging everything about your relationship to Ed. Reflecting in this way will help you gain the knowledge that the past is in the past. You can move forward with compassion for yourself, choosing to do things differently as you stop giving so much to Ed in the present.

In this exercise, try completing a reflection for each three-year period that you have been in relationship with Ed. (We suggest three years because it's a relatively short period of time that you can easily grasp and remember.) You can photocopy the exercise or simply answer the questions on separate sheets of paper, if you like. Go back to a time when you first noticed the hypercritical voice and the urges to focus on your negative body image. Think back to when you first started noticing that Ed was taking priority over your social relationships. As you work on this exercise, don't let your Ed mind use it as another way to beat you up. Rather, it's a way to make a decision about how to live in the reality of your life. It's about waking up, seeing where things are now, and making a conscious decision to do things differently.

Estimate the amount of money this relationship has cost. Include the amount it cost parents, insurance, and so on. Include the cost of food that you binged and purged on.

_____

_____

_____

Estimate the number of hours per week you spent with Ed as a primary focus of your attention. How much time did you focus on Ed thoughts (thoughts about what you would eat when, thoughts about your body, thoughts about ways not to eat, where you would purge, or what lies you would tell to hide your behavior).

_____

_____

_____

Estimate the amount of time others (parents, therapists, siblings) dedicated to this relationship. How many hours did people talk with you about Ed? How many hours did your family spend researching treatment options? How many hours did people spend trying to convince you to be healthy?

_____

_____

_____

Naikan can be felt to be confrontational, so you need to approach it as a quest for the truth. Remember, this is not about what you should feel guilty for; it's about realizing all aspects of your eating disorder so that you don't believe Ed when he tells you how harmless your behaviors are or that you're only hurting yourself. Using the exercises in this chapter and in the book as a whole, you will gain information and even more reason to see through Ed's lies and begin to change your life. No one can take this eating disorder away from you without you wanting to be free from it. It's your choice. Now it's time to act for a purpose.

CONCLUSION

As you can see with the exercises in this chapter, motivation is something that comes and goes and gets stronger at times and weaker at different times. Ultimately, your actions are what matters most. Through these exercises, you can become increasingly aware of your readiness for change, the reasons why you might want to hold on to your eating disorder, and the reasons why you want to recover. This step of awareness and maintaining awareness will increase your motivation to continue acting for recovery even if you think or feel like you don't want to put in the effort. You can begin to practice the skills in this workbook, and with practice you will learn how accepting thoughts, acting with purpose, and challenging Ed mind gets you motivated and helps you stay motivated.

In this chapter you've learned about the benefits of indentifying your healthy-minded purpose and how to act on it even if your thoughts, feelings, and bodily sensations tell you not to. You've learned to use the pros and cons chart to remind yourself that while your eating disorder might help you in the short term, learning skills to replace your eating disorder will help you have a life worth being present in for the long term. Through understanding the concept of Ed mind, developing empathy for the abuse you suffer with Ed, and learning ways to begin to separate from that abusive process, you'll increase your drive to be free. And the DBT skills in the following chapters will help you learn how to live that life worth being present in.

CHAPTER 4

Understanding Your Patterns

So far, we've spent some time understanding bulimia, how DBT can help, and the role motivation will play in your success. Now let's make sense of the patterns of behavior in your life that keep you locked in the cycle of bulimia. To do this, we'll use the process of behavior analysis, or chain analysis, that we discussed in chapter 2. As you may remember, behavior analysis is a process that helps you understand what happens to you and inside of you (your thoughts, feelings, and body sensations) in a step-by-step fashion. We will look at each link in a chain that leads from a prompting event, through internal experiences and other external events, to a problem behavior like bingeing or purging, and then on to the consequences of that behavior. We will also look at what factors may have made you susceptible that particular day to falling into that pattern, like a poor night's sleep, feeling ill, and so on.

HOW BEHAVIOR ANALYSIS CAN HELP

Doing this analysis can help you in several important ways. Sometimes the chains of behavior that lead to problems can happen so quickly that you might have difficulty breaking them. Learning the patterns that lead you to your bingeing and purging can help you to catch things more quickly so you aren't caught off guard as often.

For example, Linda spent a year and a half coming home most nights of the week feeling okay. But most evenings, before she knew it she was feeling terrible, raiding the cabinets, eating until she felt sick, and then purging. As she used behavior analysis, she came to understand that she actually felt pretty stressed when she got home. When her husband said little more to her than "hi," she felt worthless and had many recurrent thoughts about being unlovable. All of this led to her bingeing and then purging. When she finally understood what was happening, she could use skills to reduce her stress, talk to her husband about his behavior, and manage her thoughts differently.

Being aware of the patterns or the chains of behavior that lead to your bingeing and purging can help you feel—and most importantly *be*—more in control of them.

For instance, as Linda was working on her chains, her growing sense of control helped her to use skills to change her behavior. Understanding these behavioral chains can also help you to figure out which behavioral skills (which we'll cover later in this book) might work best to help you break the cycle.

You should also know that there are pros and cons to doing this, like there are with most things in life. In order to develop this understanding of your behavior, you will probably have to analyze your patterns over and over. It takes repetition to understand things thoroughly enough. And doing this kind of analysis is often uncomfortable. Success requires you to look at painful experiences honestly and in detail. This isn't easy for anyone to do. The benefit, though, is that as you go through this very hard process you can gain greater freedom from the thoughts, feelings, sensations, and events in your life that have made you miserable.

SOME IMPORTANT TERMS

In this discussion, we'll be using some language that may be new to you (or that is used in unfamiliar ways). So let's start with some definitions, just to make sure everything is clear.

Susceptibilities. These are factors that leave you physically vulnerable to feeling bad (or what we refer to in DBT as being in emotion mind) and therefore more likely to binge or purge. Susceptibilities include sleeping too much, too little, or too poorly; feeling physically sick (with a cold or flu, for instance); or using mood-altering substances like alcohol or other drugs. These factors make it more likely that you will binge or purge, but don't necessarily lead you directly to binge or purge.

Capitulating. For instance, you might say to yourself, "Well, I already blew it today, so I might as well keep bingeing." Capitulating is using your past or potential future behavior to justify not changing or controlling your behavior in the present. It helps to keep you stuck right where you are, in Ed mind.

Prompting events. People often call these events "triggers." Prompting events are things that happen, usually external events, that cause you to feel bad. A prompting event could be something like being in an argument, hearing criticism, or seeing something that reminds you of a troubling memory. Prompting events usually happen within a few hours or minutes of the binge or purge and almost always since the last time you fell asleep. (Being asleep means you were able to have regulated your emotion; if you fell asleep and then binged, that means something prompted the binge since you woke up.) Sometimes events are really hard to identify—they may not seem like "events." For example, coming home and seeing an empty apartment can be a prompting event, especially if loneliness is very painful for you.

Links in the behavioral chain. These are thoughts, feelings, sensations, behaviors, and subsequent external events that happen *after* the prompting event. These may include feeling shame after hearing criticism, having thoughts that the criticism must be true, sitting in your living room with the lights and TV off, and so on. These links are thoughts, feelings, and behaviors that lead to the bulimic episode.

Problem behaviors. People with eating disorders will commonly say "I used behaviors," meaning their problem behaviors. For the purposes of this book, problem behaviors include restricting, bingeing, purging, and other compensatory behaviors (see chapter 1). More broadly though, this could include any problem behavior a person has.

Short-term consequences. These are the immediate consequences that follow a problem behavior, usually within a few seconds to a few minutes. They often include a positive feeling or sensation or some kind of relief from a painful feeling or sensation. Positive sensations or feelings or relief from painful feelings or sensations may follow most, if not all, binges or purges.

Long-term consequences. These are consequences that come after the short-term consequences, and they may occur within a few minutes or even a few hours. Even though short-term consequences are often positive or involve relief, long-term consequences often are painful. They may include feeling guilty, feeling shame, having thoughts that you've failed again, or an increased sense of being out of control.

TRACING YOUR BEHAVIORAL CHAINS

Now that you have some familiarity with the language involved in examining this process, you can take the opportunity to trace some of the behavioral chains you experience. We have included the Behavioral Chain Worksheet on the following pages, which will help you keep track of your behavior analyses. Make some copies so that you have them ready for other analyses that you do.

Use the Behavioral Chain Worksheet for episodes when you *only* binge, or *only* purge. If you go from bingeing to purging soon afterward, however, use the Behavioral Chain Worksheet for the binge, and then use the Compensatory Chain Worksheet to understand what happened with the purge. The Compensatory Chain Worksheet is shorter than for a full chain analysis, and will make understanding the whole episode a bit easier.

After you have done several analyses, it will be time to begin figuring out what patterns repeat over and over. For instance, were there susceptibilities that were present in most or all of your analyses? Was there something similar about all or most of the prompting events? Did you have similar thoughts, feelings, and sensations along the chain to your binge/purge? What was similar about the consequences? Understanding these similarities will improve your awareness of events that are part of a chain leading you toward bingeing and/or purging as they happen. The more aware you are of the chain as it happens, the better able you will be to prevent an episode from occurring.

BEHAVIORAL CHAIN WORKSHEET

What susceptibilities were present prior to your binge/purge? How well did you sleep? Have you restricted (not had anything to eat for over three to four hours) before the binge? Were you feeling sick? Did you use any mood-altering substances? Was there anything else that made you more susceptible to feeling bad or stressed?

_____

_____

What was the prompting event? What happened in your environment? What did you become aware of? Who said what to whom? What change occurred around you that set you on a path toward your last binge/purge episode?

_____

_____

What was your immediate reaction to the prompting event above? What did you think? What did you feel? What did you do?

_____

_____

What other links in the chain happened between the prompting event and your binge/purge episode? What other things did you think, feel, or do? What other events occurred? For each link, circle T for thought, F for feeling, S for sensation, B for behavior, and E for event. Use additional paper if you need it.

T   F   S   B   E

_____

T   F   S   B   E

_____

T   F   S   B   E

_____

T   F   S   B   E

_____

T   F   S   B   E

_____

T   F   S   B   E

_____

T   F   S   B   E

_____

T   F   S   B   E

_____

T   F   S   B   E

_____

T   F   S   B   E

_____

What happened immediately before the binge/purge episode? What did you think, feel (very important), or do (also, very important)? Did you capitulate?

_____

_____

As you binged, how did you feel?

_____

_____

Short-term consequences: Immediately after your binge, how did you feel? What did you think?

_____

_____

Long-term consequences: How did you feel later? What did you think?

_____

_____

COMPENSATORY BEHAVIOR WORKSHEET

What links in the chain happened between bingeing and your compensatory behavior? What other things did you think, feel, or do? Did you capitulate? What other events occurred? For each link, circle T for thought, F for feeling, S for sensation, B for behavior, and E for event. Use additional paper if you need it.

T   F   S   B   E

_____

T   F   S   B   E

_____

T   F   S   B   E

_____

T   F   S   B   E

_____

T   F   S   B   E

_____

T   F   S   B   E

_____

T   F   S   B   E

_____

T   F   S   B   E

_____

T   F   S   B   E

_____

What compensatory behavior did you use (purging, restricting, and so on)?

_____

_____

As you used the compensatory behavior, how did you feel?

_____

_____

Short-term consequences: Immediately after your compensatory behavior, how did you feel? What did you think?

_____

_____

Long-term consequences: How did you feel later, after the compensatory behavior? What did you think?

_____

_____

As you look back over the chain analysis from each worksheet you completed, can you think of anything you could have done differently to get you off the chain to bingeing and purging?

_____

_____

Some Helpful Tips

Here are some tips to help you with your ongoing behavior analyses.

* Sometimes it helps to start by writing down what happened during the problem behavior (binge or compensatory behavior). Work backward to fill in what happened until you get to the prompting event.

* If you are having trouble remembering, write down anything that you can recall. Ask yourself what happened just before and just after what you can remember. Fill in the links as much as you can.

* Don't worry if there isn't much you can remember on any one analysis. The more often you do these analyses, the easier it will be to remember.

* Carry a worksheet with you. Write things down as they happen. If you don't have a worksheet, take notes on any paper you have.

UNDERSTANDING OVERALL PATTERNS

After you have done at least two behavior analyses, it's time to begin to tie them together. Here is a worksheet to help you identify what common patterns show up between binge/purge episodes. Make copies first, so that you can revise your understanding over time.

YOUR BULIMIA PATTERNS

Typical susceptibilities:

_____

_____

_____

_____

Typical prompting events:

_____

_____

_____

_____

Typical feelings along the chain:

_____

_____

_____

_____

Typical thoughts along the chain:

_____

_____

_____

_____

Typical sensations along the chain:

_____

_____

_____

_____

Typical behaviors along the chain:

_____

_____

_____

_____

Other typical events along the chain:

_____

_____

_____

_____

Typical feelings just before you binge:

_____

_____

_____

_____

Typical short-term consequences of bingeing:

_____

_____

_____

_____

Typical long-term consequences of bingeing:

_____

_____

_____

_____

Typical thoughts, feelings, sensations, behaviors, and events before compensatory behaviors:

_____

_____

_____

_____

Typical compensatory behaviors:

_____

_____

_____

_____

Typical short-term consequences of compensatory behaviors:

_____

_____

_____

_____

Typical long-term consequences of compensatory behaviors:

_____

_____

_____

_____

CONCLUSION

In this chapter, you learned more about how a behavior progresses by doing a chain analysis of your bingeing and purging behavior. You completed a worksheet to analyze a specific episode of bulimic behavior, and you learned some tips to help you recognize what happens in the chain of behaviors. After doing two analyses, you filled out a worksheet looking at the overall pattern of your bingeing and purging behavior. Going through these steps will lay the foundation for you to be able to use the skills that we will discuss in the coming chapters to change these problem behaviors.

CHAPTER 5

Mindfulness Skills

In the last chapter, we took a look at how to understand the patterns of behavior in your life that lead to bingeing and purging. In this chapter, we will start introducing you to skills that will help you break these chains of behavior. More than that, because bulimic behaviors can serve as solutions to other problems (as we discussed in chapter 2), these skills can offer you new ways of dealing with the problems that led you to binge and purge in the first place.

Julia used behavior analysis to understand that her binges functioned to reduce feelings of fear and being overwhelmed after stressful days on the job. She figured out that when she saw she had many things left undone on her to-do list at the end of the day, she would leave work feeling very emotional. After she got home, bingeing relieved her of fear and the feeling of being overwhelmed. When she started thinking about how much she had eaten though, this quickly led to feelings of being out of control and anger at herself. Purging gave her relief from these feelings in the short run, but later left her feeling ashamed and guilty.

As she learned how to use DBT skills, she gradually broke this cycle. Julia used mindfulness to improve her awareness of stress and fear at work and on her way home. On days she felt fearful and overwhelmed as she got home, she used emotion regulation skills to help her feel better. When her feelings were very intense, she used distress tolerance until her urges to binge had fallen off.

Some days she had difficulty preventing a binge and overate despite her efforts. On those days, she used emotion regulation skills again to help herself with feelings of anger and being out of control. She practiced acceptance skills to cope with having binged. In accepting, Julia recognized that she had done her best and that she didn't want to make things any worse—not even if purging gave her temporary relief. She then returned to her resolve to act on her purpose.

With hard work, her binges and purges happened less and less often. Julia became better at regulating her feelings without using bulimic behaviors. She also noticed something else. She had started to use DBT skills in other areas of her life. She recognized that she had started using more skillful behavior at work. Mindfulness skills helped her make better use of her time. Distress tolerance and acceptance skills helped her realize that things often remain undone at the end of the day, despite her best efforts. She also used interpersonal skills to negotiate more effectively. Overall, her level of distress in life had gone down and she felt more competent.

Julia's example illustrates the different types of skills taught in DBT and how they can work. In the following chapters, we will look at ways of practicing and learning mindfulness, emotion regulation, interpersonal, and distress tolerance skills. Each chapter will have worksheets and practice exercises to help you learn the skills.

There will be a lot of material in the next several chapters because there are many skills to learn. The more skills you have available to you, the better prepared you will be to address your problems effectively. Take your time practicing the skills. Only through lots of practice will you benefit from the skills you'll be learning. The current ways you cope and your bulimic behaviors have very likely developed over the course of years. Be patient with yourself, and give yourself the time to learn these new behaviors. Your patience and effort *will* pay off for you in the long run.

WHAT IS MINDFULNESS?

People commonly talk about "being in the moment" or "being in the flow." These ideas refer to the capacity that we all have to be fully present in life. When you can be wholly present, several things can develop for you. Life can feel more fulfilling. There can be a surprising richness in the opportunity to live more deeply more of the time. As you become more aware, you can be ready to make the best choices possible at any given moment. Rather than acting automatically or out of habit, you can respond more effectively to the challenges that life presents. Moreover, although it might seem right now that being more aware of the problems may distress you further, the kind of awareness that is cultivated through mindfulness practice can actually foster greater mental calm.

Take a moment to think about the following questions:

- In the shower this morning, did you actually feel the water as it washed over you?

- When you stepped outside, did you notice the difference in air temperature outdoors?

- If you stopped to buy some coffee, did you notice what the cashier looked like?

- Did you talk on the phone today while you were doing something else?

- If you went to work or elsewhere today, how much of the scenery along your route did you actually see?

A commonly used definition of mindfulness has three important parts. Mindfulness is *awareness* of the *current moment* with *acceptance* (Germer, Siegel, Fulton 2005). Let's look closely at each one of these elements. One definition of awareness is "consciousness, recognition, and realization." Mindful awareness is more than just sensing something. It involves sensing things in a conscious way so that you recognize and realize what is going on. For example, the last time you went grocery shopping, you might have absentmindedly put things into your cart. You may have found yourself in the snack aisle and grabbed that bag of chocolate chip cookies without really weighing whether or not that choice was a good one. Or you might have sensed a passing thought that maybe it would be better for you to pass on buying the cookies. Using mindfulness, you would have fully been conscious of what you were doing, recognizing the choice you were making and realizing what was important to you. Aware of all this, you could have acted on your purpose and left those cookies behind.

Mindfulness practices and the skills that go with them have been used for thousands of years in almost every culture on earth to help people out of suffering and misery (Goleman 1988). Mindfulness skills are the core skills in DBT (Linehan 1993b). They are considered the core because, with increased awareness in each moment, you have increased choice. Increased awareness and choice make it easier for you to use any skill you know, and this includes any other DBT skills you learn. The easier it is for you to use skills, the easier it will be for you to solve problems in life and change the patterns of bulimic behavior that have been troubling you.

Being fully aware won't necessarily help you if you are drifting in a daydream, deeply lost in a past memory, or anxiously worrying about what might happen in the future. That's where the current moment comes in. Life is happening *now*. The actions you take right now will have consequences for you. Distress that you feel now can be giving you important information that can help you to make effective choices. Worrying about what has happened or what might happen is painful. The past is done—learn what you need to learn from it and live your life now. What you worry might happen might not ever occur. Acting with awareness now can help you have the best future you can. Worrying about the past or future can keep you from awareness of things that can be rich and fulfilling right now. So awareness of the current moment is crucial to mindfulness.

Finally, you can be aware of what is happening right now and be in complete misery over it. Pleasant experiences can be easy to accept. If you've ever gotten good news, like you were due a large refund on your taxes, did you ask yourself, "Why me?" Did you curse fate or get angry with the IRS? Of course you didn't. But acceptance of painful situations is much harder. If, after getting your refund, you learned that you had made a mistake on your tax forms and had to pay the money back, you would probably be upset. That would be painful. If you then started to tell yourself that you were stupid for making the mistake, got angry at the IRS for making their forms so complicated, or wracked your brain for a way to lie your way out of the situation, you would probably prolong your pain or make it worse. In that case you would have added misery to your pain.

Have you ever heard the phrase "Pain is inevitable, but misery is optional"? That's what the acceptance piece of mindfulness is about. Mindfully being aware of your problems doesn't save you from pain—nothing really can. Life will be painful at times. But mindfulness can release you from misery and suffering.

Pain vs. Suffering

So what is the difference between pain on the one hand and misery and suffering on the other? If you stub your toe, the physical pain you experience is inevitable. It is our nature to feel physical pain with an injury. Misery and suffering come in when you get angry with yourself for being clumsy, when you get angry at whoever put that table where you could hit it, or when you worry about how long the pain is going to last. Similarly, let's say a friend makes a critical remark to you and you feel hurt. It's human nature to feel hurt when you encounter certain types of criticism. Misery and suffering arise when you spend the next several hours going over in your mind what your friend said, think about other critical comments others have made to you, and miss your turn on the expressway because you've been so preoccupied. Pain is what happens in the moment when something unpleasant happens; misery and suffering follow when you think or do things that keep you hurting after the moment has passed. Mindful awareness of problems means letting go of blaming yourself or others and letting go of useless anger, guilt, and shame. At the same time that it can release you from suffering, mindful awareness of problems can help you to see them clearly so that you can learn from them. When you can learn, you can act differently in the future.

This is a complicated topic, and we will return to these ideas when we discuss emotion regulation and acceptance skills. And, of course, what we are talking about here takes a lot of work. The changes that mindfulness can bring will accrue slowly. As you work on the following skills, remember that practice, practice, practice is important.

MINDFULNESS SKILLS

Now that we have talked a bit about what mindfulness is and what it can do for you, let's take a step-by-step approach to learning how to actually do mindfulness. Many mindfulness teachers and approaches begin with awareness of the breath. Your breath is always with you. When you practice mindfulness of breathing, you don't have to do anything special—it can be done virtually anytime, anywhere. Breathing is also an interesting place to start because it's a behavior that's usually pretty automatic but can be voluntary at times.

Mindful Breathing

So let's do some practice right now. Sit down in a chair and place both of your feet flat on the floor. Sit upright, with the bones in your spine supporting your weight as much as possible. Sit in a relaxed way but stay alert. You might imagine a thread connected to the crown of your head and extending directly upward. Keep your spine in line with the thread so that you sit straight but not stiffly. After you read the instructions, allow your eyes to rest on a neutral spot in front of you, at about a 45-degree angle down from horizontal.

1. Find a place in your body where you feel your breath. It might be where the air enters and leaves your nostrils. It might be the feeling of the air at the back of your throat or the rising and falling of your shoulders, chest, or abdomen.

2. Allow your attention to rest gently in that spot.

3. Notice how breathing feels. The point is not to think about it, but to really feel it.

4. Just allow yourself to breathe naturally. Don't make your breath special in any way. It doesn't have to be deep or slow, shallow or fast.

5. Notice when your attention wanders. It may wander to sounds, thoughts, memories, sights, or other sensations.

6. Notice where your attention wandered.

7. Gently bring attention back to the feeling of your breath.

8. Do this over and over.

9. Practice for a few minutes. Two or three minutes is a great start. Try it for longer if you like.

What was this first exercise like?

_____

_____

What did your breath feel like?

_____

_____

Was it easy to notice the feeling or your breath, or was it difficult?

_____

_____

How much did your mind wander—a lot or a little?

_____

_____

What did your attention wander to?

_____

_____

Did you notice any judgments about the exercise? If so, what were they?

_____

_____

Here are three other simple mindfulness practices you can use.

- Count your breaths from one to ten: one on the in breath, two on the out breath, three on the in breath, four on the out breath, and so on. When you notice your mind wandering from your breath, return your attention back to counting at one. Even if you never get past one or two, you're being effective if you stick to your commitment of bringing your attention back to one when you notice your mind wandering. You might notice that you get to "eleven." If that happens, you can just notice that you weren't focused on counting your breaths because you didn't stop at ten and bring your attention back to one.) Simply bring your attention, nonjudgmentally, back to one.

- You can focus on the pause between inhalation (in breath) and exhalation (out breath). As you breathe, pay close attention to the pauses between your in breath and your out breath. When your mind wanders, simply notice it nonjudgmentally and bring your attention back to the pauses.

- You can do a triangular breathing exercise. As you breathe, count up to ten as you inhale, count to ten as you hold your breath, and then count to ten as you exhale. You can change the speed at which you count to make the exercise comfortable.

Also practice mindfulness of your breath as you think of it or as it seems helpful throughout the day in your regular activities. You can research the many, many mindfulness exercises available to find others that will work for your practice. The goal with this practice is that it becomes more familiar so that you can slip into a mindfulness state of mind and be increasingly mindful and present from moment to moment in your life.

People have a wide range of reactions to mindfulness practice. It may be difficult, or it just may seem pointless. When you begin to think about practice being difficult or hard, notice how that feels. These words often make people want to give up trying because they think mindfulness practice is too difficult. In reality, the experience is just unfamiliar, and with lots of practice it will become familiar. We urge you to continue to practice, even though negative thoughts about the process may crop up. You can notice the urges to want to give up because mindfulness feels so unfamiliar, and then you can bring your attention back to practicing. Just notice the thoughts, feelings, and sensations that pull you away from your practice; realize they are just thoughts, feelings, and sensations (not fact); and bring your attention back to the practice. As you practice, you may find your mind quieting down. This will make mindfulness practice both more familiar and comfortable and more valuable to you. Be prepared to have different experiences each time you settle down to practice mindfulness. Your practice may go from feeling difficult to feeling easy, or vice versa, and back again. You can notice those judgment thoughts (deciding the experience is difficult or easy) and bring your attention back to your practice. Try to approach mindfulness with curiosity and interest.

Noticing: Just Observing Your Experience

The first exercise was what you might think of as a formal mindfulness practice. You sat down and sat still specifically to practice mindfulness. However, part of the real usefulness of mindfulness is that you can apply it in daily life. This is where the skills come in. Rather than just sitting in silence, you use these skills in everyday activities. At the same time, it's helpful to learn each of these skills in formal practice. Doing this will make you more comfortable with them and more likely to use them later.

You already learned the first skill, actually. When you noticed how your breath felt, you were practicing noticing. *Noticing* is about directing your attention, but it's also taking just a little step back, internally. Stepping back can help you see things more clearly (Gunaratana 2002).

Imagine you are at a parade. Rather than watching the parade from the sidewalk, however, you are right in the middle of the marchers. You aren't really marching with them and aren't part of the parade; you're just wandering a bit aimlessly. There are baton twirlers, clowns, and all sorts of people in costume coming at you. Everything is a blur. You are actually getting bumped around a lot. This is sometimes how life can feel.

Now step out of the parade. Step up on the curb. Observe what is happening in the parade. You can imagine that you would feel a bit calmer. You can now truly see what's going on. You are noticing what is happening without being carried away by it. You might even imagine that you can rise up above the parade in a balloon. Now you can still see the parade, you aren't being carried away by it, and you can see there is more going on in the world than just the parade. Stepping back to varying degrees is what noticing can be like.

One other thing about noticing merits mention before we discuss some ways to practice. Noticing is like having a nonstick surface in your mind. Let's say that while you're noticing your breath, a thought that is upsetting arises. When you aren't practicing noticing, you might spend a lot of time with that thought. Maybe it's about something embarrassing that happened. You might start to judge yourself, criticize yourself for getting into that situation, or think about how others were unfair. But since you're practicing noticing, as soon as the thought comes up you simply note it and then let go of it as best you can. You don't spend time with it, analyzing or debating it. You don't even try to push it away. You just allow it to begin and end without putting energy into it. A nonstick pan accepts whatever food you place in it without rejecting it or clinging to it in any way.

Noticing in Everyday Life

Here are a number of ideas for practicing noticing in your everyday life. Choose a few and do them over the next few days:

- Find other aspects of your breath to practice noticing with. Use the examples we offered in the first exercise as a guide: the feeling of the breath as it enters and leaves your nostrils, the feeling of the air at the back of your throat, the rise and fall of your shoulders, chest or abdomen, and so on.

- Do a body scan. Start at the top of your head. Notice any sensations you find there. Slowly move your attention downward. Notice sensations for each part of your body—your face, neck, shoulders, arms, and so on. Observe if you get stuck on any parts of your body or if you skip over any of them.

- Practice noticing sounds. Just notice the sounds inside and around you. Notice how they come and go. If there's a sound that seems more constant, like the heating or air conditioning, listen closely to it. Notice how almost every sound is constantly changing.

- Try noticing with your vision. Find one object—a flower, a painting, or something else with details. Notice what you see.

- Notice with your vision by just looking around at all the objects that surround you. See color, texture, and shape. Observe movement.

- Practice noticing your thoughts. This can be difficult to do. Work at allowing your thoughts to pass like cars on the street. Don't stop them. Don't jump in and go for a ride. As you get better at noticing thoughts, you'll see that your thoughts may come frequently, but they aren't strung together as much. They become much less like a dialogue or a monologue than just collections of ideas that come and go like cars on the highway.

- Notice your thoughts as thoughts, rather than as facts or truths. Notice that you can have a thought that the sky is orange with green stripes just as well as you can have the thought that you are now on planet earth. One you immediately believe is false, and one you believe is true. Practice noticing your thoughts not as things that are true or false, but just as things that occur in your mind.

- Practice noticing your emotions. Become aware of what you're feeling right now. Observe the actual sensations in your body that are part of that feeling. Notice tightness, heaviness, lightness, warmth, cold, and anything else that accompanies an emotion.

These are just a few ways of practicing noticing. Do your best to try all of them. Use them to generate your own ideas. Even more importantly, once you've started using noticing in formal exercises, use this skill as you go about daily activities. Practice observing as you wash the dishes, pay your bills, or talk to a friend.

Using Your Thoughts Mindfully: Labeling Your Experience

Labeling is just what it sounds like: using your thoughts to describe what you are experiencing mindfully (Gunaratana 2002). This can be harder than it seems. Most of the time we add interpretations, judgments, and assumptions to what we experience. This is actually what we do with our thinking almost all of the time.

For instance, say a colleague is walking down the hallway toward you. You say, "Hi," but she doesn't respond. You immediately start thinking that she must be upset with you. You search your mind for what you must have done and start to tell yourself you're a failure as a coworker. You start to feel very ashamed and angry with yourself.

Have things like this happened to you? Let's look more closely at this situation. Unless there is more information here than we've discussed, you made some assumptions, interpretations, and judgments. All that really happened in the situation is that you greeted your colleague, and she walked past. She could have been preoccupied. She might not have heard you. She might have been embarrassed herself about something she thought she did to you and was avoiding you because of it.

From the standpoint of mindfulness, though, you said, "Hi," and she walked by. Using the skill of labeling, you would look at your thoughts in just this way. You would stick to the facts and let go of anything extra. This doesn't mean that at some time you wouldn't try to figure out what happened and perhaps talk to her about it. It does mean that, in the moment, you would label the situation, stick to the facts, let go of interpretations, assumptions, and judgments, and definitely not act as though those interpretations, assumptions, and judgments were the truth.

Using our earlier example of being at a parade, after you step up on the curb, simply label what you are seeing. Imagine saying to yourself, "Clowns...trombone players...drummers...," and so on. A different example is a sports announcer on the radio who describes the action in the game well enough that you can understand what's happening. This is the skill of labeling.

Labeling Your Experience

Each of the exercises you used to notice your experience can also be used as a labeling exercise. While you practice, simply work at describing each experience as you become aware of it. For instance, in observing your breath, label the sensations you feel as you breathe: "Coolness at the nostrils...shoulders rising...tension in chest...warm air flowing out the nostrils...shoulders falling." Do the same for each exercise. For labeling thoughts, you might try saying to yourself, "I'm having a thought about work," or "A thought about my colleague just arose within me," or simply, "Thinking about bills."

Living Life Mindfully: Engaging in Your Experience

We have a number of phrases for the kind of experience where a person is fully and completely involved in what they're doing. This happens when you are in a conversation, immersed in an activity, or absorbed in whatever you're doing without worrying about your performance, questioning yourself, or being somehow self-conscious. Mihály Csíkszentmihályi, a psychologist who has studied optimal experience, has called this flow (1990). Some people also call this being in the zone or being in the moment. There can be a sense of effortlessness and ease in this state, even while doing something difficult. This is not the same thing as doing something mindlessly—you are definitely aware of what you're doing.

We will call the skill or ability to do this *engaging*. Common examples of this include a musician who's skilled at her instrument. She has practiced the musical piece that she's playing well enough that all of the notes and passages come to her without effort. She is fully aware of her instrument, her fingers, and the sounds she's making. There are few, if any, thoughts that come between her and what she's doing. If she makes an error, she continues to play without missing a beat and without self-criticism. Another example is a skilled athlete. In the middle of the action of play, he's aware of his body, aware of his opponent's body, and aware of his goal. There is no time to strategize or second-guess. In his awareness of what's happening, seeing an opportunity to score and taking it are one and the same.

These are examples of people skilled at doing challenging things. Whether or not you see yourself as being skilled in a particular activity, you likely have had similar experiences. You don't have to play an instrument or be an athlete to have been in the moment or engaged. There are many everyday things people do that require great skill and engagement, even if most of us don't recognize them as such. For instance, have you ever been in a very engrossing conversation? A conversation where you were intensely focused on what was going on? Maybe the rest of your surroundings seemed to fade away. Maybe you were even in a noisy environment, like a busy restaurant, but the busyness around you had little effect on what you were saying. Have you ever gotten so engrossed in a movie that you were laughing and crying with all the characters? Or maybe you've been involved in a puzzle, doing some knitting, reading a book, or doing dozens of other things where you were one with what you were doing. It might have lasted for some time, or it might have just happened in short bursts. Even if you've only had this experience for very brief moments, this is the skill of engaging.

Learning to Engage

Take some time now to think about a time when you were engaging. Answer the following questions:

What activity were you engaging in, even for a short while?

_____

_____

During the time you were engaging, do you remember thinking a lot, or were your thoughts few and far between? What do you remember thinking about?

_____

_____

While you were engaging, did you have a sense of the activity being difficult or a sense that you were struggling, or did you have a sense of relative effortlessness or even pleasure? What do you remember feeling?

_____

_____

Take some time now to think of a time when you definitely were not engaging. Answer the following questions:

What activity did were you engaged in?

_____

_____

During the activity, do you remember thinking a lot, or were your thoughts few and far between? What do you remember thinking about?

_____

_____

While participating in the activity, did you have a sense of it being difficult or a sense that you were struggling, or did you have a sense of relative effortlessness or even pleasure? What do you remember feeling?

_____

_____

If you were able to come up with examples, notice the differences between the two experiences above. Engaging in your life is one of the most important skills in DBT and can be your most useful route to dealing with bulimia and other problems. Living in an involved and skillful way as much and as often as you can will bring you more of what you want and need in life.

Of course, it takes work to get there. When learning new skills and learning how to respond differently to old problems, you will need to take many steps. The mindfulness skills we have examined so far can often be used in a sequence. For example, you probably need to work at noticing what happens when you tend to get upset in a certain kind of situation. It may then be helpful to be able to use labeling to be clear about what happens and what the facts of the situation are. This is part of what you did when you practiced behavior analysis in chapters 2 and 4. Labeling will help you be aware of what's happening in the moment. It can also help you as you use new behaviors and skills. Once you've practiced the new behaviors and skills and they become more natural for you, you can use engaging.

Engaging in Your Life: Further Exercises

Take a moment to list some activities that you have some skill at. Examples might include singing, knitting, doing crossword puzzles, playing tennis, drawing, playing video games—just about anything. You don't have to know how to do any of these activities perfectly, be a champion, or otherwise be an expert in any way.

1. _____

2. _____

3. _____

4. _____

5. _____

6. _____

7. _____

Next, take some time this week to practice using engaging with each activity. Give yourself at least a few minutes where you throw yourself into each activity. Be mindful of what you are doing. Let self-criticism, doubts about your performance, self-criticism, and other worries pass through your mind without letting them stick. Sometimes it helps to do the activity for a while without concern about engaging. Notice the thoughts that go through your mind. Notice whether your attention wanders. Then use engaging. Notice any differences. Keep track of what you notice below.

Activity 1: _____

If you tried the activity without engaging first, or if you shifted in and out of engaging, what was your experience like when not engaging? What were you thinking and feeling?

_____

_____

When you used engaging, what was your experience like? What were you thinking and feeling?

_____

_____

Activity 2: _____

If you tried the activity without engaging first, or if you shifted in and out of engaging, what was your experience like when not engaging? What were you thinking and feeling?

_____

_____

When you used engaging, what was your experience like? What were you thinking and feeling?

_____

_____

Activity 3: _____

If you tried the activity without engaging first, or if you shifted in and out of engaging, what was your experience like when not engaging? What were you thinking and feeling?

_____

_____

When you used engaging, what was your experience like? What were you thinking and feeling?

_____

_____

Activity 4: _____

If you tried the activity without engaging first, or if you shifted in and out of engaging, what was your experience like when not engaging? What were you thinking and feeling?

_____

_____

When you used engaging, what was your experience like? What were you thinking and feeling?

_____

_____

Activity 5: _____

If you tried the activity without engaging first, or if you shifted in and out of engaging, what was your experience like when not engaging? What were you thinking and feeling?

_____

_____

When you used engaging, what was your experience like? What were you thinking and feeling?

_____

_____

Activity 6: _____

If you tried the activity without engaging first, or if you shifted in and out of engaging, what was your experience like when not engaging? What were you thinking and feeling?

_____

_____

When you used engaging, what was your experience like? What were you thinking and feeling?

_____

_____

Activity 7: _____

If you tried the activity without engaging first, or if you shifted in and out of engaging, what was your experience like when not engaging? What were you thinking and feeling?

_____

_____

When you used engaging, what was your experience like? What were you thinking and feeling?

_____

_____

One Thing at a Time

We live in a culture where multitasking is encouraged and often expected (Rosen 2008). At work, filling out forms, answer calls, and eat lunch all at the same time is frequently the norm. At home, cleaning house, cooking dinner, and planning tomorrow's tasks simultaneously is considered the sign of an effective person. The consequences of this behavior, however, are seldom discussed. You may have noticed that multitasking tends to result in poorer performance on each individual task. More importantly, multitasking is stressful. Stress can make a person vulnerable to many kinds of problems, including bulimic behaviors.

Doing one thing at a time isn't a popular strategy, but there are benefits. Focusing on doing one thing at a time can improve your performance and reduce your stress level. Sometimes doing one thing at a time can even help you get a list of things done faster than if you tried to get them done all at the same time. In addition to these benefits, being focused and doing one thing at a time can help you calm and quiet your mind. We will call the skill of focusing on one thing at a time *one-pointedly* (Goleman 1988). This practice is often referred to as "one-pointedness" because you focus your awareness to a point, and that point is directed to just one thing at a time.

So far, we have discussed outwardly doing one thing at a time. It's important to understand that one-pointedness is also about keeping your mind on one thing at a time. This means that while you are washing the dishes, your mind isn't on what happened earlier in the day or what you'll be doing later. Your mind is on washing the dishes.

In short, the skill of one-pointedness can be thought of as when you are walking, walk; when you are sitting, sit; when you are eating, eat; and so on. Let's work on some exercises to help you with one-pointedness.

Operating One-Pointedly

Choose an activity that you enjoy, like watching TV, playing with a pet, or gardening. Spend some time doing that activity one-pointedly. Notice how you feel during and after the activity.

Practice one-pointedness for a few minutes each day. Decide on using one-pointedness during any activity you would normally do that day (washing the dishes, driving to work, picking up dirty clothes, and so on). Do just that activity. Don't multitask; work to keep your mind as much as possible on the task. Use the worksheet below to record what happens.

Activity 1: _____

How did you feel during and after the activity?

_____

_____

Activity 2: _____

How did you feel during and after the activity?

_____

_____

Activity 3: _____

How did you feel during and after the activity?

_____

_____

Activity 4: _____

How did you feel during and after the activity?

_____

_____

Activity 5: _____

How did you feel during and after the activity?

_____

_____

Activity 6: _____

How did you feel during and after the activity?

_____

_____

Activity 7: _____

How did you feel during and after the activity?

_____

_____

The value in using this skill and in practicing an exercise like the last one is that you build your skill at controlling your attention and directing it where you want at any one time. When you're under stress or there's a lot going on in your environment, this practice can help you maintain your focus and therefore act more effectively. It can also help you to calm and quiet your mind. When your mind is quieter, it's easier to make effective choices. You may have noticed this happening when you practiced, although it may take repeated use of this skill to experience the calming effect. Keep this in mind, and keep practicing!

Increasing Acceptance, Decreasing Misery

When we first introduced mindfulness, we said that you could think of it as awareness of the current moment with acceptance. So far, we have largely been discussing awareness of the current moment. We will have much more to say about acceptance when we cover distress tolerance skills (Linehan 1993b), but we will get a head start right now by discussing being aware without judgment by using equanimity (Germer, Siegel, and Fulton 2005; Nhat Hanh 1975). *Equanimity*, as we will be using the term here, refers to the ability to approach both desirable and unwanted situations with the same state of mind. In being able to do this, you can bring all your faculties and abilities to all situations, rather then doing your best when you feel good and struggling when you don't.

Judgments have a useful place in life. We definitely have to exercise the use of judgment in choosing a good job, place to live, place to go to school, and many other important things in life. These types of choices often work most effectively when we look in detail at what each choice offers us and what the likely consequences are of making a particular choice. For instance, we might choose a job based on a combination of how the demands of that job might match our skills, the compensation offered, the benefits offered, how far it will be to commute, the kind of atmosphere we might find at work, and a host of other considerations. When talking to others, we might, in a shorthand way, say it's a good job or a bad job without having to necessarily explain all the details (Linehan 1993b).

It may be obvious, but it's important to point out that saying to another person that we thought a job was bad, without explaining the details, would leave that person without an understanding of exactly why it was bad. This isn't necessarily a problem, except that we resort to this type of shorthand quite a bit of the time. Think about how many times today you might have said or thought that something was bad or good. Many of us do this without a clear understanding of exactly what made us label something as good or bad. For example, you might say that you are good at tennis. But what exactly makes you good? Do you have a strong serve? Do you have a solid backhand? Maybe you understand this clearly, but perhaps you don't. Or you might say that you're bad at math. Do you know exactly what makes you bad at it? Do you lack a strong understanding of the laws of mathematics? Do you tend to rush through complicated problems and make errors because of it? And why does this lack of clarity even matter?

It matters because if you know what makes you good at something, you can make the best of your strengths. If you know what makes you bad at something, you can work at getting better or compensate for your weaknesses. The movement away from judgments and toward details can give you important information. If you just say you're bad at math, do you necessarily know how to improve?

So one way of looking at this is that using the precision of equanimity will help you to be more in contact with what's happening. By using shorthand, you necessarily leave out what may be important information. Becoming aware with equanimity of the current moment can make you better able to respond effectively.

Moreover, when people make judgments, they are more likely to respond with stronger emotions to what they are judging. Think about the last time you said something was bad. More than likely, you experienced at least just a little bit of distaste, aversion, irritation, or maybe even disgust. The stronger these emotions are, the harder it is for us to really understand what we're facing. Even positive judgments can interfere. The presence of positive emotions can also make it harder for us to realistically evaluate choices. Think of a time when you or someone you know was in a relationship with someone who was "really great," but it became clear that you or they were overlooking a lot of problems.

There's an old Zen story about a farmer and his son that can illustrate some of the points we're making. One morning after a terrible storm, a wise old man was taking his morning walk into town on his usual route past the corral of a neighboring rancher. On this particular morning he met the rancher, who was repairing the fence around his corral. The wise man asked what had happened, and the rancher explained that the storm had frightened one of his stallions. The horse bolted into the fence, destroying it and freeing all of his other horses. The rancher lamented this by saying what a very bad thing this was. The wise man answered by saying, "Bad, good—it is hard to say." The wise man continued on his way, and the upset rancher had no idea what to make of this statement.

During the wise man's next daily walk, he approached the rancher, who was beaming with happiness. When asked what made him happy, the rancher pointed to his corral, saying that his stallion had returned with all of his horses and several wild mares as well. The rancher concluded by saying this was a good thing indeed. The wise man answered again, "Good, bad—it's hard to tell."

The next day, the wise man encountered another development as he passed the rancher's corral. The rancher was again quite distraught, and he explained that his son had tried to ride one of the wild mares and was thrown to the ground, breaking his leg. The rancher complained that this was very bad, a terrible thing that had happened. Once again, as you might have guessed, the wise man said, "Bad, good—it's hard to tell." Also, as you might have guessed, the rancher was starting to have his fill of the wise man's craziness.

Well, on the next day, the wise man passed the rancher's corral again. This time, the rancher was quite exuberant. The wise man asked how the rancher's son was, and the rancher explained that the army had come through yesterday, forcing young men into their ranks under threat of execution. They had to pass the rancher's son over, however, because of his broken leg. The rancher cheered that this was a very, very good thing for sure. The wise man responded, of course, by saying, "Good, bad—it's hard to say." And the rancher finally understood.

Using Equanimity

One of the first steps to using equanimity is to notice when you are making judgments. Take a moment to think back over what you have said or thought today. What judgments do you remember making? Below, list as many as you can.

_____

_____

_____

_____

_____

_____

Next, keep track of making judgments over the next few days. Try to keep a rough tally of how many judgments you make, and work to keep track of what the judgments were. This can be hard to pull off, but do your best. Use the spaces below.

Day: _____ Number of judgments: _____

List: _____

_____

_____

_____

_____

Day: _____ Number of judgments: _____

List: _____

_____

_____

_____

_____

Next, let's get some practice using equanimity. Think of someone you don't like. Write down what you think of them below, without censoring what you say:

_____

_____

_____

_____

_____

_____

Now underline or circle any judgments you can identify in your statement above. Keep in mind that sometimes judgments come as evaluative words like "good," "bad," "evil," "wonderful," and "terrible," and sometimes they're implied in the emotional tone in a statement. For instance, think about the difference between saying, "I don't want to take that job" versus "I don't want to take *that* job!"

Next, try to write a statement using equanimity and explaining what makes you not like that person. Refrain from using judgmental words. Some ways to do this are by labeling, stating just the facts, or detailing the consequences of being in a relationship with that person. For example, you might replace "She's just terrible at conversation" with "She doesn't respond to what I'm talking about. She ignores it by saying what's on her mind, so I hardly ever feel like I've been heard."

Below, rewrite the statement about the person you dislike using equanimity:

_____

_____

_____

_____

_____

Try this exercise with a number of other things, people, or experiences that you don't like. Try this also with things about yourself that you don't like. Practice using equanimity by identifying judgments and changing them into labeling statements or statements of consequences. You might want to keep a separate notebook to use for this purpose.

The DBT Skills Workbook for Bulimia

Finally, let's practice using equanimity in day-to-day life. Over the next few days, work at identifying judgments as you start to make them or right after you've done so. Use equanimity to state what you want to say descriptively or rephrase what you've just said. Keep in mind that we aren't suggesting that you never use judgments again, but we suggest that you practice reducing how much you judge. See what happens and how it makes you feel. Also, remember that it's possible to judge your judging as bad. Practice seeing your judgments with equanimity if you can. Rather than thinking something like "I just used *another* judgment. I'm really bad at this!" try labeling mindfully to yourself, "A judgment has just come up in my mind." When you notice yourself judging your judgments, practice accepting the fact that you judge. Remember that all humans judge because we're encouraged to judge from the time we learn to talk. We can accept this habit of mind as we work toward changing it.

Day: _____ Number of times equanimity used: _____

List: _____

_____

_____

_____

_____

Day: _____ Number of times equanimity used: _____

List: _____

_____

_____

_____

_____

Day: _____ Number of times equanimity used: _____

List: _____

_____

_____

_____

_____

Acting Effectively

We have all had experiences where we found ourselves doing something that we knew wasn't a good idea. Sometimes we understood what we were doing wouldn't work before we took action, sometimes while we were taking action, and sometimes afterward. Think about the last time you bought something that was outside of your budget, or maybe the last time you went to the grocery store when you were hungry or stressed, realizing that wasn't the best time to go shopping for food.

We've all had other experiences where we knew we were "in the right" but understood that being right didn't make much difference. Maybe you got pulled over after driving through an intersection when you knew the light was just going from green to yellow. Even though you were convinced of this, the officer who pulled you over was convinced it had actually turned red. You argued and maybe even questioned how an officer's eyesight could be so poor. You fought back, even though at first the officer approached you with an easy manner. By the end of the exchange, she was clearly irritated and angry. And while you were arguing, you understood that there was a good chance you could get off with just a warning if you weren't so confrontational.

These are all examples of how we can act impulsively, without full awareness. On the other hand, when we can act mindfully, with full awareness, we have a greater chance of acting effectively. The mindfulness skill of acting effectively is the practice of doing what works (Linehan 1993b). Doing what works means having our longer-term goals in mind. Acting effectively is about understanding what will be best for us beyond any current impulses we might feel. Even though we may feel justified or right about acting confrontationally or too quickly, we can act in a way that's political, because that will work best (in the end) to get us what we want. This often involves letting go of self-righteousness, useless anger, and the need to prove a point.

Acting Effectively in Life

Acting effectively is one of the most unfamiliar of the mindfulness skills, so it can be more uncomfortable to practice. It requires using most or all of the mindfulness skills we've discussed so far, as well as understanding our goals, observing our impulses, and acting according to what's most effective. One way to get started is to think about a recent time when you didn't act effectively. When was the last time you acted in one way even though you knew better? Answer the following questions about that situation.

What was the prompting event for your action?

_____

_____

_____

_____

What action did you take?

_____

_____

_____

_____

What was your action based on in the moment? (Consider your emotions, feeling you were justified or right, feeling stressed, and so on.)

_____

_____

_____

_____

What were your longer-term goals in this situation that would have been important to consider before acting?

_____

_____

_____

_____

What could you have done differently that would be an example of acting effectively?

_____

_____

_____

_____

Over the next few days, practice acting effectively at least once each day. Answer the following questions for each time that you use the skill of acting effectively.

Date: _____

Situation for practicing acting effectively:

_____

_____

What would you have done impulsively or "mindlessly"?

_____

_____

_____

What did you do instead that was an example of acting effectively?

_____

_____

_____

Date: _____

Situation for practicing acting effectively:

_____

_____

_____

What would you have done impulsively or "mindlessly"?

_____

_____

_____

What did you do instead that was an example of acting effectively?

_____

_____

_____

Date: _____

Situation for practicing acting effectively:

_____

_____

_____

What would you have done impulsively or "mindlessly"?

_____

_____

_____

What did you do instead that was an example of acting effectively?

_____

_____

_____

Date: _____

Situation for practicing acting effectively:

_____

_____

_____

What would you have done impulsively or "mindlessly"?

_____

_____

_____

What did you do instead that was an example of acting effectively?

_____

_____

_____

In this last exercise, you had an opportunity to practice and see the effects of acting effectively. The idea here is that as you practice acting effectively, you will be able to achieve your goals in various situations more of the time without having as many undesirable consequences. Although using this skill might not get you your desired outcome with a minimum of negative consequences in every situation you noted above, hopefully you saw this happen in at least a few circumstances. Here again, with practice you'll be able to achieve your goals more and more often as time goes on.

Knowing and Using Your States of Mind

Living with awareness and cultivating mindfulness can help you participate in life more fully and act more effectively. The regular practice of noticing, labeling, and engaging, and doing so with equanimity and effectiveness, can also help you strengthen a particularly useful state of mind. In DBT, this state of mind is called wise mind (Linehan 1993b). In order to understand wise mind, it can be helpful to understand two other common states of mind first.

When you are feeling especially strong emotions, this experience tends to dominate your awareness and your actions. The stronger the feeling, the more the emotion influences what you think and do, as well as what you don't think and do. It can be as if the emotion has moved over into the driver's seat. You (and the rest of your abilities, experiences, and potential) have been put in the passenger seat. For instance, when you're feeling intensely angry, you're more likely to remember times in the past when you've felt angry. You will probably think of things in the future that might make you angry if they occur. You're more likely to think of things about the people you're interacting with right now that make you angry. It will be much harder to think of times when you felt something other than anger, to imagine things happening in the future that don't involve anger, and to notice things about people right now that make you feel anything other than anger. In addition, when you're feeling intensely angry, you're more likely to act on the anger than to act in a kindly or friendly way. Often, thinking and acting with anger can lead to continued or even more intense anger.

This same kind of thing can happen with other emotions—even pleasant ones. When this happens, you can think of this as emotion mind (Linehan 1993b). *Emotion mind* is that experience of your emotions being in the driver's seat. Your emotions take control, and you find it hard to do what is effective for you. Everyone gets into emotion mind sometimes, and it doesn't necessarily lead to problems. People can become overcome with sadness, anger, guilt, or shame and not have significant trouble because of it. People can also become overcome with joy, happiness, and love. This can be quite exciting. The more often emotion is in the driver's seat, however, the more likely that problems will result.

On the other hand, there are times that all of us stuff our feelings to some degree. At times, we squelch our feelings quite a bit. When this happens, although we might be acting (and able to think about things) quite logically, we lose access to our feelings. Reason is an important capacity to have. Our ability to be rational helps us to figure out problems and understand complicated situations. While having emotions in the driver's seat can lead to problems, losing touch with emotion can cut off access to important information, as well as aspects of our experience that can enrich our life and serve to motivate us to do difficult things.

When you lose touch with your feelings, we can call this reason mind (Linehan 1993b). The ability to reason is quite important, but when reason alone is in the driver's seat, we might be unable to take some important things into account. For instance, when someone acts toward you in an emotionally abusive way, you might logically consider that they didn't mean it, that there are important reasons to not take a stand about the treatment you're receiving, or that there's more to that person than the abusiveness. While any or all of this reasoning can be valid, an important part of the situation is that the abuse hurts emotionally. This pain is information that something is wrong. Feeling hurt and angry can also provide the necessary motivation to take on the difficult task of stopping the abuse. In reason mind, however, the rationale for how things are can keep you stuck in a situation where you get hurt repeatedly.

The ability to think rationally in combination with your emotions is what we will call wise mind (Linehan 1993b). In *wise mind*, you have access to your capacity to think logically and to make decisions. You also have contact with your emotions. Even though your emotions may be strong, they don't solely determine your actions. If your emotions motivate you to do something different than your logic, your logic alone doesn't rule the day. You have the opportunity to find a larger, more comprehensive way of looking at things that can take both your feelings *and* your reason into account. Additionally, you also have access to faculties like intuition and other ways of knowing and understanding what's going on and what's right for you.

Awareness of Your States of Mind

One way to begin the practice of entering into wise mind more often in life is to increase your awareness of whatever state of mind you are in at any given moment. This very moment, right now, is a great opportunity to start.

What state of mind does it seem you're in right now—emotion mind, reason mind, or wise mind?

_____

If you aren't sure, and also as a check to make certain, answer the following questions:

Do you feel any strong emotions right now? If so, what are they?

_____

_____

If you're having strong emotions right now, is it difficult to follow what you've been reading? Is it difficult to answer these questions? Are thoughts related to what you are feeling going through your mind, making it difficult to read and think about anything else?

_____

_____

If you answered yes to some or all of the above questions, does it seem like you are in emotion mind?

_____

Has it been easy to read the last passages of this book? Has it been easy to answer these questions?

_____

If it has been easy to read and answer these questions, are you aware of feeling any emotion right now at all?

_____

If it has been easy to read and answer and you don't have awareness of any emotion, you might be in reason mind. As you consider your situation right now, is there anything that has happened in the last few minutes or hours that you would likely have some feelings about? If so, this is more evidence that you might be in reason mind. After reading and answering these last few questions, does it seem to you that you are in reason mind?

_____

On the other hand, are you aware of feeling emotions right now *and* being able to read and think through these questions without too much difficulty?

_____

If so, you might consider that you are in wise mind.

Logging Your States of Mind

Over the next few days, check in with yourself throughout the day. Several times during a day, figure out what state of mind you are in right at that moment. Notice if you're feeling strong emotions and if they seem to be running the show for you. Consider that you might be in emotion mind. Notice if you're acting very rationally, just "taking care of business" and remaining unaware of feeling much of anything. This may mean that you are in reason mind. Notice if you're aware of thinking logically and rationally while you're also conscious of feeling emotion, but the emotion isn't in the driver's seat. If this is happening, you may be in wise mind. Use the following worksheet to keep track of this.

Date: _____   Time: _____

State of mind you were in:

☐ Emotion Mind   ☐ Reason Mind   ☐ Wise Mind

How did you know you were in that state?

_____

_____

Date: _____   Time: _____

State of mind you were in:

☐ Emotion Mind   ☐ Reason Mind   ☐ Wise Mind

How did you know you were in that state?

_____

_____

Date: _____   Time: _____

State of mind you were in:

☐ Emotion Mind   ☐ Reason Mind   ☐ Wise Mind

How did you know you were in that state?

_____

_____

Date: _____   Time: _____

State of mind you were in:

☐ Emotion Mind   ☐ Reason Mind   ☐ Wise Mind

How did you know you were in that state?

_____

_____

Date: _____   Time: _____

State of mind you were in:

☐ Emotion Mind   ☐ Reason Mind   ☐ Wise Mind

How did you know you were in that state?

_____

_____

Date: _____   Time: _____

State of mind you were in:

☐ Emotion Mind   ☐ Reason Mind   ☐ Wise Mind

How did you know you were in that state?

_____

_____

Date: _____   Time: _____

State of mind you were in:

☐ Emotion Mind   ☐ Reason Mind   ☐ Wise Mind

How did you know you were in that state?

_____

_____

Entering Wise Mind

Now that you have had some practice identifying what state of mind you are in at any given moment, let's work on some exercises that can help you get into your wise mind. First of all, know that all of the mindfulness skills you've been learning and practicing so far can help you access your wise mind. Continue to practice them!

CLARIFYING WISE MIND

In this skill, you will ask yourself a series of questions to help you get into your wise mind:

1. First, become aware of the situation you are in. What is happening right now? Are you facing a decision? Is something unclear right now?

2. Ask yourself, "What are my emotions telling me?"

3. Ask yourself, "What is my reason telling me?"

4. Now that you know what might be in your emotion mind and reason mind, ask yourself, "What is my wise mind telling me?"

5. Wait patiently for an answer. Notice that emotion mind often throws up an answer immediately. Observe that answer mindfully and wait for what comes next.

CLEARING THE WAY FOR WISE MIND

Notice your state of mind right now. If you might be in emotion mind, practice this skill:

1. Breathe in and say to yourself quietly, "Be calm."

2. Breathe out and say to yourself quietly, "Be still."

3. Repeat this over and over. Notice if your state of mind changes.

FINDING WISE MIND IN YOUR BODY

Some people experience different states of mind in different places in their body. The notion that different parts of the body relate to different faculties goes far back into history. For example, the idea of chakras in yoga locates the faculties of mind, creativity, and intuition in different parts of the body. Practice bringing your mindful awareness to different parts of your body. Notice if your emotion mind, reason mind, and wise mind are centered in different places (Linehan 1993b).

- Become aware of your thoughts. Does your awareness seem cool, distanced, logical? Is there a place in your body where your thoughts seem to occur?

- Become aware of any emotion you're feeling. Does your awareness seem hot, tense, stormy? Is there a place in your body where your emotions seem to occur?

- Some people experience wise mind deeper in their gut (Linehan 1993b). Folk wisdom tells us to trust our gut. Bring your mindful awareness there. Does your awareness seem still, centered, calm?

- Practice with other parts of your body. Notice what happens.

WISE MIND IMAGERY

Practice using the following imagery exercises. These can be useful tools for accessing wise mind:

- Imagine a leaf being blown about in the wind. Watch it as it twists, soars, and spins. Imagine the wind quieting down and the leaf slowly settling to the ground. Watch it lie in stillness.

- Imagine yourself standing on the beach, watching the waves powerfully roll in. Next, imagine wading into the water and feeling the power of the waves firsthand. Finally, take a deep breath and go under the water. Notice that the waves continue above, but the water below is much more still and gets calmer the deeper you go.

Practice each of the preceding skills for entering wise mind once a day for the next week. Even though these exercises are probably unfamiliar to you, don't give up quickly on any of them. Different skills work better for different people. Some of these practices work well in some situations and not in others. Keep at it. Experiment.

CONCLUSION

In this chapter, you began learning some of the skills that are commonly used in dialectical behavior therapy. You learned about mindfulness practice and mindfulness skills that are part of DBT. These skills included noticing, labeling, engaging, and using your awareness one-pointedly, with equanimity, and effectively. You also learned about states of mind, how to identify them, and how to enter into wise mind. In the following chapters, you'll learn skills for regulating emotion, tolerating distress, and acting skillfully in relationships. The mindfulness skills you just learned will serve as a necessary foundation for the skills coming up. The more you can be mindfully aware of yourself, others, and your life, the better you will be able to use the rest of the skills in this book, as well as any other skill that will help you in life.

CHAPTER 6

Emotion Regulation: Learning to Coexist with Your Emotions

As you learned in the previous chapter, on mindfulness, most of us are engaged in a near-constant pursuit of feelings we see as positive and in constant flight from feelings that we might judge as negative. You have also learned that this pursuit of some feelings and flight away from others is not effective and only prevents you from living in the present. The more you try to check out from your feelings, the more likely it is that you will make your life worse. That is why learning to coexist with your feelings is a more effective option. Therefore, in this chapter we'll discuss the evolutionary purpose of emotions—why we need emotions and how even painful emotions are important. Marsha Linehan discussed the idea of an evolutionary purpose of emotions in a conference on emotion regulation (2005), and we will be using some of what we learned there in our discussion. We'll also examine how you can identify your internal experience of emotions and learn to differentiate it from other sensations, like feelings of hunger or fullness. We'll see what makes you vulnerable to emotion mind and how to decrease that vulnerability. You'll also learn how to use skills to understand if your emotional reaction and its intensity are valid or not. Once you decide if your response and intensity are valid, you can use skills to decrease your emotional suffering.

UNDERSTANDING YOUR EMOTIONS

In this chapter, we're going to be discussing seven primary emotions: anger, fear, guilt, joy, love, sadness, and shame. All other emotions that you can think of are, at the very least, related to these seven emotions.

First you must learn to understand your emotions before you can learn to coexist with them. What are emotions? Why do we have emotions? What are they good for? Emotions are basically signs and signals from our bodies to help with survival. Emotions are electrical impulses in the brain that are both innate and learned (emotional responses are in part learned). All emotions are fleeting impulses that we can also intentionally or unintentionally refire, making the emotions last much longer. So, for example, if you're angry at someone you see regularly but you haven't used skills to deal with that anger, you will likely remain angry for a long time. You might stay angry because every time you see that person, think about that person, or think about what they did, you are refiring the electrical and chemical impulses in your brain that lead to anger. If that person moves out of town and you never see them again, you have no stimulus to refire the electrical and chemical reaction in your brain, and your anger toward that person might fade. However, even if you never see them again, you could still think about them and what they did and continue to feel anger. On the other hand, using skills can help you learn to reduce your anger. By doing so, you can learn to coexist with your anger, feel less angry, or be completely free of anger, even if you see the person all of the time.

The Evolutionary Purpose of Emotions

Why do you have emotions? To really understand emotions you need to first understand their evolutionary purpose. To do this, it will help if you think about what life might have been like back in the cave-person days, maybe a million years ago. Back then, life was extremely dangerous and one's survival depended on the clan. If a cave person was separated from the clan by choice, accident, or expulsion, they were as good as dead. Once they were out of the protection of the clan, they could be eaten by carnivorous animals or be unable to hunt or forage effectively enough to survive. Our emotions evolved to help with our survival. Anger and fear evolved to keep us safe from danger. Other emotions, like guilt, shame and love, helped with social interactions and improved one's chances of staying in the protective clan.

Let's look at each of the seven basic emotions and how these emotions lead us to have urges to jump into action to ensure our survival:

- **Anger** makes a person become aggressive and increases the likelihood that the person will attack what is perceived as dangerous to make that threat go away. Anger was originally a matter of survival, as there were constant threats in the environment when human beings began to evolve.

- **Fear** leads to what is called the fight-or-flight response. When feeling fear, a person is likely to run away or hide from what is dangerous and scary, or to lash out to fend off the threat. Alternately, a person might become very still in order to escape notice.

- **Guilt** makes a person attempt to repair whatever they feel guilty about. If a prehistoric person did something that could make others in the clan upset, that person would need to attempt repair or they might get kicked out of the clan. Remember, being kicked out of the clan could mean death at that time.

- **Joy** and **love** make a person want to be around others and share with them. This is crucial to the reproduction and maintenance of a clan.

- **Sadness** encourages others to be of help. If someone in the clan is sad or depressed, others come to their support (helping to make sure they eat, taking care of children, and so on). Sadness can also motivate people to attempt to regain what is lost; for instance, to search out and find someone who has drifted from the clan.

- **Shame** makes a person want to hide what they feel shame for. In prehistoric times, if someone did something about which they felt ashamed, they would fear being kicked out of the clan. Therefore, they would be careful to hide their shameful act.

So, looking at out emotions from a historical (or prehistorical) perspective, we can better understand how essential they were to survival. However, most events that prompt emotions in modern times aren't life threatening. But we may still react to them as such because we remain hardwired for the intense emotions. What happens if you do something that someone else won't forgive or that will get you cast out of a group? It might feel life threatening at times, but the reality is that you will probably survive. Humans are social beings by nature, and there is always another group to join.

What Emotions Do for You Now

Now let's look at what emotions do for you in the modern world. Linehan astutely recognizes that we need this understanding to be able to truly appreciate emotions (1993b). She makes three important points about emotions: they communicate to and influence others, they organize and motivate action, and they can be self-validating.

EMOTIONS ACT AS SIGNALS TO YOURSELF

We feel something, and this emotional response provides information and motivates us into action. The feelings can be signals that something is very wrong or that something is very right. For example, if your partner has been coming home from work later and is more distracted and uninterested when around you, you're likely to feel fear that something is wrong in your relationship. This emotional response can be helpful if you use this internal communication to open up a dialogue with your partner. But this emotional response can become problematic if you come to the conclusion that these signals are facts, jumping to the conclusion that something is wrong without first finding out. To continue with our example, an unsubstantiated fear that your partner is having an affair could move into anger. You might then act as though your feelings are fact and respond from emotion mind. You might impulsively attack, at which point your partner might view you as irrational and possibly even dangerous, so more distance would grow between you. A dynamic like this occurs when you believe that your emotions are fact even though you don't really have any hard evidence. A more helpful way to respond would be to use the emotion as a signal to communicate with your partner and find out the truth of the matter. It could be that your partner is actually working longer hours and is distracted because of pressure to increase performance in order to get a raise.

Emotions also signal us to act more quickly when necessary. For example, if you're walking down the street and a car screeches around a corner, you're likely to reflexively both scream and jump out of the way because of fear. You don't have to think about screaming and jumping—you just do it.

EMOTIONS HELP YOU COMMUNICATE WITH OTHERS

"Nonverbal communication" is the term most often used to point out how human beings communicate through facial expressions and body language. Even if a person is saying one thing with words, their nonverbal communication can convey quite a different message. You might tell someone that you like them because you don't want to hurt their feelings, but if every time they come near you your body tenses and you look away to avoid eye contact, your nonverbal communication tells that person that you aren't interested, even if your nonverbal actions aren't within your awareness.

This nonverbal communication can also lead to mass communication. In the old days, this would be helpful in communicating with one's clan. For example, if a bunch of people are running toward you with a look of fear on their faces, you may start running with them (imagine entering a pet store after a container of tarantulas was knocked over and all the customers are running toward the door). You might read the fear on their faces and respond as if a threat is likely following them. If you don't start running, the threat might get you. However, this can be problematic if the person who started running wasn't running due to a real threat, but because they feared there was a threat. Incidents like this can lead to mass panic for no reason.

INTERPRETING YOUR EMOTIONS

So if you can't change the way humans are hardwired and you understand that your emotions are necessary for survival, what can you do if your powerful emotions feel like they are running your life? You can learn to regulate your emotions.

In order to do so, you must first learn how to interpret these internal messages. You need to become mindful or aware of what goes on inside of you when you're experiencing emotions. This is another reason why you learned mindfulness first—it truly is a core skill.

One way to check in with your emotions is to be mindful of your body's cues. When you feel an emotion, it usually has a physical component. We can use these physical signs as cues to check in with our emotions.

Take a mindful moment now and check in with your body. You can start by asking yourself, "How do I feel physically?" then move to the more specific questions below:

- Is my heart pounding?

- Am I sweating? Am I cold?

- Do I feel emptiness inside my stomach?

- Do I have goose bumps?

- Is my jaw tight? Do I have tension in my neck or anywhere else?

- Do I have butterflies in my stomach?

- Do I feel nauseated?

Mindfully tuning in to these sensations will help you become mindful of when you're feeling strong emotions and functioning from emotion mind. You'll also be better able to understand when you're sad, for example, instead of hungry, or when you're anxious, for instance, instead of not hungry. Once you're able to identify when you are in emotion mind, you can use that awareness to cue you to use your emotion regulation skills. For example, when your heart pounds, whether it is from anger, fear, love, or shame, you can take a few minutes to go through your body. You can figure out which emotion you're feeling and determine if your feelings are getting out of control. You can then use emotion regulation skills if necessary. In order to learn how to identify and understand your emotions, try the following exercise.

Getting to Know Your Emotions

For the following exercise, we'll be asking you to think back to the past. First, we want you to think back to a time when you were angry. You'll examine this past experience and answer some questions that will help you to more fully understand how it played out. Then you will do the same for an experience of fear and each of the other five emotions. After you're done completing the exercise for incidents in the past, you can do it in the present. The next time you feel any of the seven emotions, examine that experience using the questions in this exercise.

But first, let's look at an example of a situation that prompted anger and how this emotion manifested and played out. We'll use an interaction Lilly recently had with her family:

1. Lilly's mother told her that she could have the car to get to work. But then Lilly's brother, Sam, interrupted by insisting that he needed the car to get to a job interview. Lilly's mom responded by letting Sam take the car, suggesting that Lilly could catch the bus if she left right away.

2. This happened first thing in the morning, after a sleepless night for Lilly.

3. She interpreted this situation as unfair.

4. Lilly's heart pounded. She felt her muscles tense up and a sensation of heat spreading over her face.

5. As her anger mounted, Lilly felt the urge to attack her brother.

6. Lilly clenched her fists and yelled at Sam, screaming that she hated him. She then turned on her mother, yelling that her mom always gave in to Sam and that it wasn't fair.

7. After her explosion, Lilly felt guilty that she said she hated Sam—he looked really hurt. She realized that Sam hadn't heard their mom say she could have the car and that he was really nervous about his interview.

Now it's your turn. For each of the emotions listed below, think of one example in the past (recent or long ago) that you can work through. This exercise will help you to better identify and understand your emotions. The more practice you get at these skills, the more familiar they will become. Once you can adeptly identify and understand your emotions, you'll be able to use other emotion regulations skills more readily.

Anger

1.   What happened that led to the development of the emotion?

_____

_____

2.   When did the situation happen that led to the development of the emotion?

_____

_____

3.   What interpretations might have led to the development of this emotion?

_____

_____

4.   What did you experience?

_____

_____

5.   What action urge did you feel? What did this emotion make you feel like doing?

_____

_____

6.   How did you express this emotion or act on it? What did you say or do?

_____

_____

7.   What were the consequences of the emotion (both short-term and long-term)?

_____

_____

Fear

1.   What happened that led to the development of the emotion?

_____

_____

2. When did the situation happen that led to the development of the emotion?

_____

_____

3. What interpretations might have led to the development of this emotion?

_____

_____

4. What did you experience?

_____

_____

5. What action urge did you feel? What did this emotion make you feel like doing?

_____

_____

6. How did you express this emotion or act on it? What did you say or do?

_____

_____

7. What were the consequences of the emotion (both short-term and long-term)?

_____

_____

Guilt

1. What happened that led to the development of the emotion?

_____

_____

2. When did the situation happen that led to the development of the emotion?

_____

_____

3.   What interpretations might have led to the development of this emotion?

_____

_____

4.   What did you experience?

_____

_____

5.   What action urge did you feel? What did this emotion make you feel like doing?

_____

_____

6.   How did you express this emotion or act on it? What did you say or do?

_____

_____

7.   What were the consequences of the emotion (both short-term and long-term)?

_____

_____

Joy

1.   What happened that led to the development of the emotion?

_____

_____

2.   When did the situation happen that led to the development of the emotion?

_____

_____

3.   What interpretations might have led to the development of this emotion?

_____

_____

4. What did you experience?

_____

_____

5. What action urge did you feel? What did this emotion make you feel like doing?

_____

_____

6. How did you express this emotion or act on it? What did you say or do?

_____

_____

7. What were the consequences of the emotion (both short-term and long-term)?

_____

_____

Love

1. What happened that led to the development of the emotion?

_____

_____

2. When did the situation happen that led to the development of the emotion?

_____

_____

3. What interpretations might have led to the development of this emotion?

_____

_____

4. What did you experience?

_____

_____

5. What action urge did you feel? What did this emotion make you feel like doing?

_____

_____

6. How did you express this emotion or act on it? What did you say or do?

_____

_____

7. What were the consequences of the emotion (both short-term and long-term)?

_____

_____

Sadness

1. What happened that led to the development of the emotion?

_____

_____

2. When did the situation happen that led to the development of the emotion?

_____

_____

3. What interpretations might have led to the development of this emotion?

_____

_____

4. What did you experience?

_____

_____

5. What action urge did you feel? What did this emotion make you feel like doing?

_____

_____

6.   How did you express this emotion or act on it? What did you say or do?

_____

_____

7.   What were the consequences of the emotion (both short-term and long-term)?

_____

_____

Shame

1.   What happened that led to the development of the emotion?

_____

_____

2.   When did the situation happen that led to the development of the emotion?

_____

_____

3.   What interpretations might have led to the development of this emotion?

_____

_____

4.   What did you experience?

_____

_____

5.   What action urge did you feel? What did this emotion make you feel like doing?

_____

_____

6.   How did you express this emotion or act on it? What did you say or do?

_____

_____

7.   What were the consequences of the emotion (both short-term and long-term)?

_____

_____

As you go through this exercise with each emotion and continue to practice this exercise, your ability to identify your emotions will become more natural and effortless. To use the emotion of shame as an example, your increased mindfulness of your emotions will help you more quickly pick up cues that you're feeling shame when you begin to experience it. You'll be able to examine the interpretations you made to contribute to your feelings of shame. You'll recognize the internal physical experience of shame and the action urges that accompany it. You'll also be able to use skills more effectively to not withdraw and isolate because of the shame. And you might prevent yourself from getting angry with others as an aftereffect of your shame.

CYCLES OF EMOTION

Now that you can understand how to interpret your emotions, you can also see how an emotion develops and travels through a cycle. Marsha Linehan offers a "model for describing emotions" (1993b, 137) in which she talks about prompting events for emotions, interpretations, brain changes, face and bodily changes, an emotion name, and the aftereffects. A similar life cycle of an emotion is described here, and we'll go into it in greater detail below. Consider a strong emotional experience that you've had in the recent past as you read about this progression.

There is typically a *triggering event* for the emotion: What happened that led to the development of the emotion? What was the triggering event?

There are *physiological vulnerabilities* to the emotion (created by not paying attention to one's biological or physiological needs): What biological factors, present before the triggering event, contributed to the development of the emotion or to its intensity? Were you tired, hungry, and so on?

There are *thoughts*, *beliefs*, or *interpretations* that come from the trigger and are skewed and strengthened by the physiological vulnerabilities: What thoughts or interpretations might have led to the development of this emotion?

There's an *emotional experience* that's a combination of a physiological response and an urge to do something in response to that physiological response. For example, Sharon often experiences tightness in her stomach that comes from anxiety, and she has the urge to go for a run and skip her lunch because of that tightness. What did you experience physically? How did your body experience the emotion? Then, based on what you experience, there's an internal urge to react to your experience (refer to the evolutionary purpose of emotions earlier in this chapter for common urges that are associated with the seven individual emotions). How did you express this emotion? What did you say or do?

Finally, there are *consequences* of your emotion and your response to that experience: What were the consequences of the emotion (both short-term and long-term)?

If you can understand the life cycle of the emotion, then you can understand how and when to apply emotion regulation skills. Now that you are more able to identify your experience of each emotion, let's learn how to coexist with them instead of trying to pursue "positive" emotions and run from "negative" ones.

ATTENDING TO PHYSIOLOGICAL BALANCE

As we briefly mentioned in chapter 4, everyone has certain physiological needs that must be acknowledged and met in order to function most effectively. If you don't pay attention to your human biological or physiological needs, you are significantly more likely to be in emotion mind. The physiological vulnerabilities are biological factors, present before a triggering event, that contribute to the development and maintenance of an emotion, as well as its intensity (Linehan 1993b). As you begin to recognize the differences between your different mind states and learn to understand the physiological factors that can make you more susceptible to emotion mind, you can begin to develop more empathy for yourself, as opposed to impatience. Think about a young child that you care about. If that child is hungry or tired, for example, what does that do to the child's mood? How often have you heard someone comment, "Oh, the baby needs a nap. She's getting cranky"? The child's physiological needs are acknowledged, accepted, and recognized as contributing to the negative mood state. Not only are these physiological needs of the child accepted, they are also quickly soothed. Unfortunately, somewhere along the way we lose that empathy for adolescents and adults. Physiological vulnerabilities continue to be a major factor in the moods and functioning of adolescents and adults, but society tells us to ignore them. Unfortunately, ignoring these biological necessities not only makes you more susceptible to thinking emotionally, it also keeps you in that emotional place. In order to increase your ability to stay out of emotion mind, you need to attend to your physiological balance. Extremes on either end aren't healthy and can increase your susceptibility to the extremes of emotions.

Now let's take a closer look at each of the physiological factors that can impact your mood and emotional intensity. The vulnerabilities we've chosen to focus on come from Marsha Linehan's work (1993b): hunger, fatigue, illness, and substance use.

Hunger

The healthiest way to keep your body fueled is to eat something nutritionally well-balanced every three to four hours throughout the day. Consider again the hungry baby. Most parents make sure that their child eats every few hours or they expect some emotional fallout. Even though you are now an adult, you still have a pressing biological need to allay your hunger. If you ignore your body's hunger signals, you become more vulnerable to emotion mind. If you go for longer than three or four hours, your metabolism begins to slow down, and then your body isn't functioning as effectively. This also sets you up to binge. You reach a point after three or four hours where your body gets so hungry (whether you acknowledge it or not) that when you do finally eat, you're more likely to feel a loss of control and binge. Likewise, if you're eating every hour because eating temporarily takes your mind off of your emotional pain, you're making yourself more vulnerable to emotion mind. The overeating or bingeing can lead to physical pain or feeling sick, which can then make you more prone to emotion mind. In this case, you might also feel shame (as a secondary emotion) about the eating once the short-term relief passes.

To determine how you tend to your body's need for food, try using the following food record to track your eating patterns for one week. Please make at least seven photocopies of the blank form before you begin filling it out so that you can complete it every day for the next week.

When filling out the food record, you might feel the internal pressure to change how you're eating because you know you have to write it down and see it in black and white. You may realize that you're likely to judge yourself and feel afraid to be as honest as possible because you don't want to see how "badly" you are eating (judging yourself or your eating as "bad"). Try to keep in mind that the food log is simply a tool to help you understand your eating patterns. It isn't about judgment. You're gathering information to help you feel better, not as evidence of how badly you handle food intake.

To fill out the daily food record, write the day of the week and the date on the top. Under "Food Intake," write down everything that you consume (including alcohol, water, and *anything* else you put into your body). For example, after filling out the food log for a week, Mike realized that he was much more likely to binge after smoking marijuana. Write the time that you began to consume in the "Time" column. Under "Location," write down where you were when consuming (for instance, in front of the television, in the car, at the dining room table, and so on). If you believe it was a binge, check the "Binge" column, and if you purged, check the "Purge" column. Finally, under the "Situation" column, write down what was going on at the time. For example, maybe you were thinking about an argument with a friend, were with your significant other who was critical, or were talking with an ex on the phone.

Daily Food Record

Day: _____   Date: _____

Time	Food Intake	Location	Binge	Purge	Situation

Once you've filled out this food record for a week, can you see how your mood is impacted by your eating, and how your eating is impacted by your mood? What patterns do you see emerge? Did you have any periods in which you didn't eat for longer than four hours? If so, did it impact your mood? Did you binge following a period of restricting food for four hours or more? How did you feel immediately after you binged? How did you feel an hour after you stopped bingeing?

Fatigue

Just as a small child gets cranky and is prone to emotional outbursts if she doesn't get enough sleep, so are you. The healthiest way for an adult to sleep is to get seven to eight hours of sleep a night. If you're getting less than that or your sleep is interrupted, you're more susceptible to emotion mind. Likewise, if you sleep more than eight hours a night you're likely staying in bed for reasons other than sleep, and staying in bed will only increase your emotional dysregulation. We acknowledge that adults have varying sleep needs, as some people require more sleep and some people need less. It's best to tune in to your body to see how much you need and use that for guidance. Filling out the following sleep log can help you make a wise-minded decision as to what number of hours of sleep is most effective and healthiest for you.

Fill out the following sleep log for a week and see how your mood is impacted by your sleeping. Rate your mood on a scale of 1 to 10 with 1 as feeling the most emotionally regulated and 10 being totally emotionally dysregulated. What patterns do you see emerge? Did you have any periods in which you got less than seven or eight hours of sleep? If so, did they impact your mood and your bulimia? Did you sleep more than eight hours? If you find that you could use more or better-quality sleep, try these sleep hygiene tips:

- Establish a regular sleep schedule (go to bed and wake up approximately the same time every day).

- Don't nap.

- Don't consume caffeine (coffee, caffeinated sodas, lots of chocolate, and so on) after noon.

- Don't use nicotine or alcohol in the evenings.

- Get regular moderate exercise early in the day, but avoid exercise in the evenings.

- Don't go to bed hungry or after very heavy meals.

- Have the bedroom be a quiet, dark, cool, and comfortable space.

- Create a routine in which you have time to decompress before bedtime (mindfulness exercises can help).

- When thinking about worries or frustrations in bed, redirect your attention to other things. (Mindfulness of counting one's breath can be effective for this purpose.)

- When you can't fall asleep, get out of bed. Only return to bed when you feel drowsy.

Illness

Consider the emotional fussiness of a sick baby. He doesn't feel well, which makes him much more prone to explosions of emotion or general weepiness. It's the same for adults, so maintaining good health is important for your emotional well-being.

Weekly Sleep Log

Day and date	Time you got into bed	Time it took to fall asleep	Number of awakenings after falling asleep	Time you got up for the day	Total hours of sleep	Napping: Time of day and duration	Total nap time during the day	Fatigue rating during following day (1 as least fatigued, 10 as most)	Average mood rating for the day

The healthiest way to fight illness is to get plenty of rest (seven to eight hours) and to eat in a nutritionally balanced way throughout the day. If you exercise when you're physically sick or in pain, you're likely to make your illness or injury worse. The decision to continue exercising when you're unwell might be coming from emotion mind. We don't put an emphasis on exercise in this book because many people with bulimia nervosa overexercise to compensate for calories consumed or for calories they plan on consuming. There are well-known emotional and physical health benefits to exercise. However, if you're struggling with bulimia, exercise can become one of your problem behaviors. Therefore, we recommend that you discuss your exercise regimen with a health professional knowledgeable about eating disorders.

When you do get sick or experience any kind of physical pain or discomfort, you are more vulnerable to emotion mind. While it is very understandable that illness or pain can lead to emotional dysregulation, you likely don't recognize this dynamic as it occurs. If you can become aware that the illness or pain is increasing your susceptibility to emotion mind, then you can have empathy for yourself and be ready to use your other skills when you notice the impact on your mood. When experiencing any physical discomfort for longer than a day or two, you should see a physician to see if you need treatment. If you recognize your discomfort as temporary (you have a headache or a stomachache, for example), do your best to remedy the discomfort while giving yourself empathy for the pain. You might even speak to yourself (in your head) as though you were a child, using comforting words to express empathy and care. This can go a long way toward soothing your feelings when you're in pain.

Substance Use

The healthiest way to think and feel is to do so without substances. Any mood-altering recreational substances (from nicotine and caffeine to alcohol and marijuana to heroin and crack cocaine) severely impair your ability to think clearly. Even prescription drugs can impair your functioning if you don't use them as prescribed. When your ability to think and feel clearly becomes impaired due to mood-altering substances, you're much more susceptible to emotion mind and to acting ineffectively.

Mindful Scan of Physiological Balance

So now that you understand the physiological human needs that must be addressed to decrease your susceptibility to emotion mind and the need to attend to your physiological balance, try this scanning exercise. In an emotional moment, do a mindful scan of yourself and check your vulnerabilities.

Did you eat healthfully today, or have you restricted or binged?

_____

Did you get at least seven to eight hours of sleep last night? Have you been sleeping well lately? Have you been sleeping more than necessary?

_____

Are you physically sick or in pain? Have you been pushing yourself physically?

_____

Have you consumed any mood-altering substances? Are you taking your medications as prescribed?

_____

How is your balance? Is any physiological need out of whack? Once you have a better understanding of what factors make you more susceptible to emotion mind, you can begin to have some empathy for yourself when you find yourself in that state. Instead of judging yourself ("Why did I overreact? I am so sensitive and emotional!"), you can now acknowledge your situation with more accuracy, less judgment, and increased empathy ("I got only five hours of sleep last night. Of course I'm feeling emotional. I need to take care of myself"). When trying to recover from bulimia, it's crucial that you learn to become aware of why you are in emotion mind, because this is the state of mind where you'll encounter Ed mind.

ED LIVES IN EMOTION MIND

Through years of treating people with eating disorders, it has become clear that one of the hurdles to overcome when attending to physiological balance is that people with eating disorders don't want to accept that they are, in fact, human and that because they are human, they have physiological needs. When you don't attend to your physiological balance, using your DBT skills is like playing piano with one hand tied behind your back. How can you expect that your human body shouldn't have the basic needs of any other human? If you do, that's a solid sign that Ed is in charge, because it really makes no sense. You *are* human, and that is a reality that must be accepted, even though Ed tells you otherwise. If you can embrace the fact that you're human, then you can accept that you need to take care of your human body in order to function effectively.

Our client Annie once wrote:

> Something that stuck with me since the last session was when you mentioned how when I want to use Ed, maybe I could see that as an opportunity to have empathy for and take care of myself instead of hurting myself. That is a very big difference in my mind, and I tried it the other day. It proved to be pretty effective. I wanted to binge, but then I realized that I was really stressed-out and tired. I decided to take a bath instead and try to relax. It helped.

Recall from chapter 3 that Ed mind is like an internal abusive commentary. Ed mind grows in strength when you don't attend to your physiological balance and are more susceptible to emotion mind. Ed mind will also increase the likelihood that you'll make decisions from emotion mind that throw off your physiological balance, making you more prone to emotion mind. For example, when you're feeling tired and hungry you're more likely to misinterpret and then get upset by your partner not calling. Ed will then tell you that your partner doesn't love you and will never love you because you're so fat. Ed will tell you that you shouldn't eat all day in order to make yourself thinner and more lovable. You then restrict all day because Ed mind is very convincing. Restricting throws you more out of balance, as it makes you more tired, and being tired and starving make you even more susceptible to being in and acting from emotion mind. When you're more deeply rooted in emotion mind, you're likely to respond to your partner in a way that pushes them away (by being desperate and needy or cold and angry). This might make your partner more aloof, and then Ed jumps in to show you how right he was.

We have just one question for you: How is this dynamic working for you? Does listening to Ed mind help you, or does it keep you more trapped in Ed mind and emotional suffering? Once you are really aware of the vicious traps constantly set by Ed, you can more effectively manage to stay away from them. There is a wonderful poem by poet Portia Nelson (1994, 2-3) that might help you understand why awareness is imperative.

AUTOBIOGRAPHY IN FIVE CHAPTERS

1. I walk down the street.
   There is a deep hole in the sidewalk.
   I fall in.
   I am lost… I am helpless.
       It isn't my fault.
   It takes forever to find a way out.

2. I walk down the same street.
       There is a deep hole in the sidewalk.
       I pretend I don't see it.
       I fall in again.
   I can't believe I am in this same place.
       But, it isn't my fault.
   It still takes a long time to get out.

3. I walk down the same street.
   There is a deep hole in the sidewalk.
   I *see* it is there.
   I still fall in…it's a habit…but,
       my eyes are open.
       I know where I am.
   It is *my* fault.
   I get out immediately.

4. I walk down the same street.
   There is a deep hole in the sidewalk.
   I walk around it.

5. I walk down another street.

Listening to and acting from Ed mind is like falling into the hole. You may be oblivious to it, but with attention and effort you can learn recognize it. You have to be willingly aware of the hole, consciously decide to not step in (using your bulimic behaviors) even though it is habit, develop new habits (DBT skills), then choose a totally different approach (learning to coexist with your emotions instead of trying to run away from them). Now try this exercise to assess your level of awareness of the "hole" of Ed mind.

Trying a New Path

Reread Portia Nelson's poem and think about your level of awareness of the hole. Think about the hole as being in an emotional state of mind that leads to listening to Ed mind. Write about what each stage feels like as you go through it.

1. What was or is it like being the person in the first stanza, lost and helpless? Is that where you are now?

    _____

    _____

2. What was or is it like being the person in the second stanza, pretending the problem isn't there? Is that where you are now?

    _____

    _____

3. What was or is it like being the person in the third stanza, habitually doing the same thing even though you can begin to recognize that falling in the hole doesn't help you? Is that where you are now?

    _____

    _____

4. What was or is it like being the person in the fourth stanza, still vulnerable to falling into the hole and willing to walk around it? Is that where you are now?

    _____

    _____

5. What was or is it like being the person in the fifth stanza, taking a totally different route, switching from an ineffective path to an effective one? Is that where you are now?

    _____

    _____

Now think about what it would take for you to move through the stages of the poem, the stages of recovery. Many people can get to the third or fourth stanza, and then they find themselves stuck. You can see the hole, and yet something keeps pulling you back into it (Ed mind). This is where your skills can really come in handy. You must first be aware (mindful) that you are standing by the hole, and then you must be in wise mind to choose to go around it or take an entirely different street.

SKILLS TO REGULATE YOUR EMOTIONS

Now you understand several important aspects of emotions. You've learned that emotions are electrical impulses in the brain that are both innate and learned and that all emotions are fleeting experiences that we can also intentionally or unintentionally refire, making the emotions last much longer. You have read how this contributes to the cycle of emotions. You understand how to recognize your emotions, why we have emotions, why they're necessary for survival, and the importance of attending to your physiological balance. Now it's time to look at what to do with emotions when you're feeling dysregulated or when your emotions are otherwise contributing to you doing things or making decisions that make things worse. You are *emotionally dysregulated* when you have difficulty controlling your actions because of the intensity of your emotion. In this section, you'll learn how to determine if your emotional response or the intensity of that response is valid, given the facts. You'll learn how to use skills to be mindful of your emotions without judgment and how to focus on experiencing positives. Finally, you'll learn the effectiveness of doing the opposite of your emotional urges.

Evaluating the Validity of Emotions

Emotion dysregulation can obviously cause many problems. A potential problem arises when an emotion or its intensity isn't valid. One definition of *valid* is "well-grounded or logically correct." Basically, an emotion or its intensity isn't valid if it isn't grounded in fact or logic. We use the term "valid" or "invalid" not to suggest that you're wrong or "crazy" for experiencing an emotion that's invalid in view of the facts of the situation. The term is simply meant as a cue to check in with the realities involved, allowing you to decide whether the emotion you're experiencing and its intensity make sense when you consider the facts of the situation.

Let's consider our client Annie. When Annie was in emotion mind she became very jealous if her boyfriend talked to another girl. In wise mind, Annie realized that her boyfriend had never cheated on her, had been with her since high school, and had made it clear that he plans on marrying her. She is able to see that he will have all kinds of friends. What really made her jealous was that Ed mind was telling her she wasn't good enough for her boyfriend, that all other girls were better than her, and that of course he would cheat on her because she wasn't worth the effort to be faithful. You can see why Annie's boyfriend would be confused about her strong jealousy—he didn't know what was going on in Annie's mind. It's important to note that an emotional response can sometimes be *understandable* (meaning that you can understand why the situation would lead to that emotion, given the interpretation) but not *valid* (meaning that the emotion isn't coming from the actual facts of the situation, but more likely from interpretation).

For example, you might feel shame about having an eating disorder (this is something we often hear from people with bulimia). This sense of shame is understandable, because you judge yourself for your behaviors, and Ed mind tells you everyone else will judge you too. However, the shame isn't truly valid (meaning that it's not based in fact), because you will most likely not be kicked out of your social group if people find out that you have an eating disorder. In fact, after years of hiding their disorder and shame, many people with bulimia are surprised at the support they receive from loved ones when they finally do reveal their struggle. So once you realize that your emotional response or its intensity isn't valid, it's time to use your emotion regulation skills.

You can get a head start on the process of evaluating the validity of emotions by trying out the exercise that follows.

Evaluating the Validity of Emotions

When feeling emotionally dysregulated, you need to look at the facts to determine validity. You can learn how to objectively assess emotional validity by considering the factors involved. Use the questions below to help with this evaluation.

What triggered your emotional response?

_____

Does your emotional response fit the event that triggered it? (Use the list of emotions and situations that trigger them from the section on the evolutionary purpose of emotions and the section on getting to know your emotions.)

_____

Are your interpretations grounded in fact?

_____

Would anyone else in the same situation make a similar interpretation?

_____

Are there other possible interpretations? What are they?

_____

_____

Can you problem solve the situation? This would mean that you would be able to figure out an action that you could take to improve or rectify the problem situation.

_____

What is the intensity of your emotion on a scale of 1 to 10, with 1 being not at all and 10 being the most intense you've ever experienced?

_____

Would anyone have a similar intensity level in a similar situation? If not, how different is your level from where you think others would be?

_____

As you go through this exercise you can see how familiar it can be to believe your emotional thoughts are truth, even though emotional thoughts are not likely to be based in truth and fact. When you actually ask yourself these questions (especially if you can do it from a more wise-minded place), then you can more accurately evaluate the validity and intensity of your emotional reactions. Once you know if your emotional response and intensity are valid or not, then you can make a decision as to what other emotion regulation skills to use next.

Being Aware of and Present with Your Emotions

A major step in regulating your emotions is to be truly mindful of them in the moment (Linehan 1993b). As you recall from the chapter 5, you need to know the mindfulness skills of noticing, labeling, and engaging to be mindful. You will now apply these skills to your emotions. While applying these skills, try to also use the other basics of mindfulness—being aware with equanimity and one-pointedness and acting effectively. Now let's try using mindfulness skills with your emotions. You can start by noticing your emotion and trying to label it, and then you can engage with your emotion.

Noticing your emotion. Simply notice your experience of the emotion. It is there. You are experiencing it. Notice what it feels like without judgment and with equanimity. Notice this without applying words to the feeling, instead simply experiencing. Focus on your experience. Just be aware of what's going on in your body.

Labeling your emotion. This means putting words to your experience. So in your head, you might think that the sadness you're feeling is like a weight on your chest. You can just notice and label this feeling without judgment. Anxiety can feel like tightness in your stomach. What do your emotions feel like from an objective, unattached point of view?

Engaging with your emotion. Accept yourself in the experience of this emotion. The experience isn't good or bad. It is simply your current experience, and it is tolerable. It's important to be aware that your experience, whatever it is, *is* tolerable, even when your thoughts tell you it's not. Remember that thoughts are just thoughts. If you respond to your thoughts as though they were facts, you'll be acting on all of your urges.

The ability to be aware of and present with emotions will also help you know when you need to use your other emotion regulation skills. As you become more familiar with mindfulness in general, and especially with mindfulness of your emotions, you will more easily engage in mindfulness when your emotions are dysregulated. Then you can use your other skills to regulate your emotions. One skill that you can use is to control where you focus your attention.

Attention and Experience

Now try this mindfulness exercise to help you understand how your attention changes your experience of pain (whether emotional or physical pain). You will see how your mind might try to distract from pain by wandering. You can experience how the feeling of pain fades when you don't focus on it, and how it gets stronger when you refocus on it.

With your thumb and index finger, pinch the underside of your opposite upper arm moderately hard. Release. Now, for the next five minutes, focus your attention on the area that you just pinched. Don't pinch it again, just notice the feeling after you pinched it.

After you have done the exercise, answer these questions.

How was the exercise for you? What did you notice?

_____

_____

What did you notice when your attention wandered?

_____

_____

Did you notice that when your attention wandered from the back of your arm, it seemed as though the feeling decreased?

_____

Did you notice that when you brought your attention back that the feeling was stronger?

_____

This exercise can show you how your attention can dramatically change your experience of not only physical pain, but emotional pain as well. Focusing on pain makes it feel more intense and causes it to last longer. To further demonstrate the power of attention, imagine being in a room that's pitch-black.

Now imagine that you have a flashlight and that the beam of light from the flashlight is your attention. If you shine the light only on the experiences that you might view as negative, you will only see the things in your life that you experience as negative. Focusing solely on the negative will increase your emotional dysregulation. If you shine the light around the room, other things will come in and out of focus. You can choose to shine your light on those things that you might experience as more positive. This can increase your emotional regulation. Remember, when you focus on pain, the pain feels more intense and it lasts longer. If you get distracted from the pain, you might even forget about it until you refocus on it.

As you might be gathering, controlling your attention by choosing what to focus on is an emotion regulation skill. When your mind wanders to the negative, you can choose (by moving your flashlight) to focus on the positive. Please keep in mind that it is an equally important skill to be able to focus on pain and know that you can tolerate it instead of trying to run away from it or avoid it. We know that constant efforts to escape pain by chronically distracting away from it can actually augment a person's experience of pain. However, if you get trapped in emotion mind because of pain and you can't problem solve it or change your interpretation of it, then redirecting your attention temporarily away from the pain can be very effective.

Likewise, when your mind focuses on worries, also choose (by moving your flashlight around the room) to redirect your attention. When Cara used to go on vacation, her mood began to deteriorate after one or two days. She explained that would start getting sad that the trip would be coming to an end. Being focused on the end of her trip prevented her from being able to enjoy the last three days of her vacations. Now when she goes on vacation and notices sad thoughts arising about the vacation ending, she redirects her attention to enjoying the moment she's experiencing. Similarly, when Annie tried to relax and have some fun, she would hear her learned internal messages that she has to deserve positive experiences. These thoughts would ruin her positive feelings. Ed has always been ready to let her know she doesn't deserve anything positive—ever. Annie is now learning that thinking about whether she deserves something or not interferes with her ability to enjoy and be present for positive experiences.

Margaret provides another example of worries that can come from positive experiences actually hampering the ability to enjoy the positive experience. Margaret does really well academically. She's an English major at the top of her class. No matter how many successes she has on her papers and in her classes, every A she earns makes her feel more pressured to do the same or better the next time. This thinking prevents her from being able to enjoy and be proud of the achievement. In fact, this pressure often contributes to the desperation that drives her to binge and purge.

There are many stories of people who lose a bit of weight through more "negative" experiences like illness, a renewed interest in exercise, or growing depression and anxiety, for example. If you relate to this, you might realize that as you lost weight, others began to comment on the weight loss. You then might have felt pressure not to regain the weight because you didn't want to lose how the acknowledgment and compliments made you feel. This desperation (worry thoughts from emotion mind) can lead you to Ed for help.

Worry Thoughts

Now take some time to write out some of the worry thoughts that might prevent you from getting the most out of positive experiences:

_____

_____

_____

_____

_____

_____

When you have these worry thoughts in the future, you can notice them, recall that they only decrease your ability to get the most out of the positive experience, and redirect your attention away from those worry thoughts. Linehan noted the effectiveness of turning away from worry thoughts as you try to increase positive emotions (1993b). With awareness of these potential blockades to getting the most out of your positive experiences, you can work on focusing your attention away from the worries.

You might say that you can't think of anything positive to focus your attention on. If that's the case, you need to begin to experience more short-term positives in your life. Another great option is to learn to be more aware of what you already experience in life but don't notice or recognize as positive, like putting on a favorite perfume (Linehan 1993b).

Experiencing Short-Term Positives

Think of things that you view as positive—not as a judgment, but as a preference. Think of things that make you smile or experiences that you enjoy. Think of things that increase your positive emotions and don't involve your eating disorder (no exercise, no food treats, and so on). For example, Cara likes to make beaded jewelry, play with her cat, take baths, smell potpourri, and listen to classical music, just to name a few.

Write down fifteen things that are positive experiences for you:

1. _____

2. _____

3. _____

4. _____

5. _____

6. _____

7. _____

8. _____

9. _____

10. _____

11. _____

12. _____

13. _____

14. _____

15. _____

Next time you feel emotionally dysregulated, you can either refocus your attention by thinking about these positive experiences, or you can add to your positive experiences by doing a few of the fifteen things you listed above. It's important that you do at least one thing every day that you can be mindful of as a positive experience. This one thing can be as big as taking a vacation or as small as putting lovely smelling lotion on your hands and mindfully experiencing the soothing sensations.

Short-term positives are necessary but not sufficient. You also need to work on building long-term positives so that you want to continue being present in your life. If you want to be present and fully experience your life, you won't need to use your bulimia to check out. To build this life, you need to set goals (the purposes in your life) and work toward them. It's important to note that, as you work toward those goals, you must break the long-term goals into smaller, more easily achievable steps. Working on these steps can help you build a sense of confidence. Starting out too big can lead to the urge to give up. Think of babies and the process they must go through to learn to walk. Typically, they must first master rolling over, then creeping, then crawling, then pulling up, then cruising while holding onto furniture, and *then* walking. All goals can be broken down in this way.

Breaking Down Your Goal

Choose one your goals and write it here.

_____

_____

Now break it down into smaller parts. You can begin with something like looking up a phone number and then making a call to gather information. Break down your goal into linear steps toward long-term positives. It might be most effective if you can break the steps down in the order that they will be performed. If you need more space, go ahead and do this exercise on a separate sheet of paper or in a notebook that you can refer to later.

1. _____

2. _____

3. _____

4. _____

5. _____

6. _____

7. _____

8. _____

9. _____

10. _____

As you work toward creating and experiencing more positives, both short-term and long-term, you'll have more to see when you shine your flashlight around the pitch-black room. This isn't to say that you should only focus on positives all the time. We all need to be aware of all parts of our reality and know that all reality is tolerable. We cannot emphasize this enough! From a mindfulness perspective, much of the misery that people experience in life comes from not knowing that emotional pain is tolerable. We will talk much more about this in chapter 7. Acknowledging that, it's also important to build more positive experiences so that you have more positives to see when you need to balance your attention. Building positives is just one skill out of many.

Now that you know how to address your physiological needs, empathize with yourself when in emotion mind, be mindful of your emotions, and create more positives to focus on when you're in emotion mind, you can learn how to use the skill of doing the opposite of your emotional urges (Linehan 1993b). This is a skill to use when you realize that you are in emotion mind, your emotional response is unjustified, and you want to shift your emotional state.

Doing the Opposite of Emotionally Motivated Urges

What do you do once you realize that your emotional reactions to a situation aren't really valid, even though they might be very understandable? If your emotional response isn't justified, how do you help yourself feel something more appropriate to the situation? For example, Katie had been going out with her boyfriend for about a year. He broke up with her, and he made it clear that they would never get back together. He told her that they just had too many differences and he knew they had no future. Because Katie still loved him, she chose to be around him whenever possible, even though this caused her emotional pain from being continually rejected by him. One day they were at a party and he told her that he missed her sometimes. Katie became so wrapped up in her excitement about this that she decided to have sex with him. She was in emotion mind, operating purely from the hope that he would miss her enough to get back together. The next day he clarified that he'd had a lot of fun with her, but he still saw no future for them together. However, he added that they could still be friends.

Although Katie wanted to be around her ex-boyfriend because she loved him, he made it clear that he didn't love her. In this case, her love might be understandable, but it wasn't valid and or justified. Her love wasn't justified because her feelings weren't requited, and they would bring her nothing but further pain. Every time Katie felt rejected by him, she would use her bulimia to cope with the terrible feeling she had about herself. She would binge and purge to numb out. However, the calm she felt after purging would inevitably fade, and Katie would focus on her romantic feelings for her ex again.

What could Katie do to help herself so she won't feel bad about this all of the time? She could act the opposite of her emotionally motivated urges (Linehan 1993b). This means that if your emotion or its intensity isn't valid in the situation, you can do the exact opposite of what you feel like doing based on your emotion. Getting back to Katie's situation, her understandable but invalid emotion is love, and the action urge for love is to approach, be close to her ex, and have regular contact. Therefore, doing the opposite of her emotional urges would be to stop spending time with him, not remain friends (which she would only do in hopes of getting him back, and the facts don't support that as a possibility), and definitely not spend time thinking about him lovingly. With time, if she uses opposite action, Katie's feelings of love will decrease in intensity and open her up to the possibility of meeting someone else.

In Alcoholics Anonymous, they have an expression that is similar to doing the opposite action: "Fake it until you make it." Many people have an emotional response to this idea, complaining that they want to be genuine and don't like the idea of "faking it." If you agree with this, you are likely responding to the judgment that you attach to faking it as being disingenuous. However, in this situation it's not about being real or false; it's about using skills to help you have a life worth living in the present. If you act opposite to how you feel when your feelings aren't justified, your feelings will decrease.

It's important to note two things about acting opposite to your emotionally motivated urges. The first is that you have to do it *all the way* (Linehan 1993b). Katie won't be able to reduce her love if she physically stays away from her boyfriend but keeps close to him in her mind. She has to do it all the way. The second thing to remember is that you have to do the opposite of your emotional urges over and over. Katie won't be able to get over her ex if she sometimes acts opposite to her urges but gives in to them at other times. In order for this skill to work for her, she has to remember to do it as often as possible, and every time if possible.

In the long run, doing the opposite of your emotionally motivated urges will help you to live a more effective life when your emotions or their intensity aren't based in truth or logic. Using this skill will help free you from the emotional upheaval that can interfere with effective living.

So what would it look like to do the opposite of your emotionally motivated urges with the seven emotions? To get a hint, you can look at the section on the evolutionary purpose of emotions. Recall that each emotion leads you to have urges to jump into action. In prehistoric times, this quick action helped ensure survival. Nowadays, these reactions to dysregulated emotions often undermine quality of life.

Acting opposite to your urges is not the same as pretending your emotion isn't there. Your emotion *is* there, and it definitely needs to be accepted. The trick is to acknowledge and accept the invalid emotion while acting opposite to the emotionally motivated urges associated with it. Looking at the chart below, you can see that each emotion leads to an emotionally motivated urge to act and also see examples of action you could do that's opposite to that urge. You must first identify what emotion you're experiencing, and then you can use the chart to help you figure out how to act in a way that opposes your emotion-minded urges.

Acting-Opposite Chart

Emotion	Emotionally Motivated Urges	Doing the Opposite
Anger	Attack, criticize, yell, hurt the other person.	Validate, distract, speak quietly.
Fear	Avoid, physically shrink away.	Approach what is feared. Do what you want to avoid.
Guilt	Confess, avoid, isolate.	Accept what you did and let it be. Continue doing what you were doing. If the guilt is justified, make reparations.
Joy/Love	Desire to be around others and share yourself with them.	Subtly avoid the person and resist sharing yourself with them.
Sadness	Shut down, avoid, do nothing, withdraw and isolate.	Get active, set goals, socialize.
Shame	Keep things secret, hide, punish yourself.	Talk about it openly and accept it.

Now think back to some recent instances when you acted on your unjustified emotions, then complete the following table. While you complete the exercise, try to be aware of how effective it is for you to act on your emotionally driven urges versus acting the opposite to what your emotionally driven urges tell you to do.

Acting on Emotional Urges

Emotion and trigger of that emotion	Emotionally motivated urges (What did you feel like doing? What was your action urge?)	What did you do?	What could you have done instead? (Doing the opposite of your emotionally motivated urges)
Anger			
Fear			
Guilt			
Joy or Love			
Sadness			
Shame			

When working on acting the opposite to emotionally motivated urges, it's important to remember that opposite action is for use with *unjustified* emotion. If, for example, you are truly in your wise mind and realize you are in physical danger (fear), leave the situation! You are certainly right to ensure your safety. On the other hand, people often live in fear that they will feel emotional pain. Emotional pain isn't the same as physical danger. The only way to reduce your fear of experiencing emotional pain is through doing the opposite of your emotionally motivated urges.

Acting the opposite to your urges can feel very unfamiliar, so many people initially believe they can't do it. Please give this skill a try, even if it feels uncomfortable at first or you feel afraid to follow through. Remember, thoughts are just thoughts. They aren't facts. Thoughts only become facts when you act as though they *are* fact. When you use opposite action, you might have the urge to give up midway because it feels so different from what you're used to. But it's crucial that you follow through when you use this skill. This means that you must do it until the emotions begin to shift. If you notice thoughts or feelings that you should stop fighting and follow your urges, just notice those thoughts and feelings and bring your attention back to using opposite action. Your persistence will result in the ability to handle your emotions and reactions in a more healthy and helpful way.

CONCLUSION

In this chapter you learned about the evolutionary purpose of emotions (why we need emotions and how even painful emotions are important for communication and to initiate action). You began the practice of identifying your internal experience of emotions and accepting your emotions as they are. You learned what makes you vulnerable to emotion mind and how to decrease that vulnerability. You also acquired some powerful skills that will help you determine if your emotional reactions are justified and then choose an appropriately intense response if the emotion is valid. If you can see that your response or its intensity isn't valid, you can use skills you learned in this chapter to decrease your emotional suffering. As your emotional suffering decreases, you'll be freer of Ed mind and emotion mind, and you won't feel the urge to use your bulimic behaviors to help you numb out, avoid, or escape your feelings. You'll know that you can tolerate your feelings and embrace being fully present in your life.

CHAPTER 7

Learning to Tolerate Feelings of Distress Without Making Your Life Worse

As human beings, we all have certain commonalities, no matter who we are and what we do. We experience peace and joy at some points in our lives and distress at others. When we experience joy, it's rare that we can't accept the good that is happening to us. For example, if a friend invites you to a party, you probably won't wonder why that friend invited you or why this is happening to you (unless you dislike parties). However, what if a friend is having a party and doesn't invite you? Then you *are* likely to question why you weren't invited. You might even have thoughts like "My friend wouldn't do that" to deny those distressing feelings. Most of us put in great efforts to avoid feeling distress and to escape it when we do feel it.

AVOIDING DISTRESS

How do you deal with your "bad" feelings? Bingeing and purging are often described as coping mechanisms for distress. (This is much like substance abuse, self-harm, and any other maladaptive behaviors that help a person escape their reality and disconnect from their feelings.) People frequently describe feeling numb or state that they go to sleep after a binge/purge episode. But bingeing and purging are an ineffective way to escape distressing feelings because ultimately they make your life worse, so you then have more distressing feelings to deal with, which leads back to the bingeing and purging to escape those feelings. You can get caught in a downward cycle that has no end. In this cycle, you might lose touch with friends because you get so consumed with running from your feelings. Likewise, you might have trouble performing on the job or in school as your focus on weight and body image takes over your life. When human beings are in emotional distress, we have four basic options for how to handle that distress. At a conference on emotion regulation, Marsha Linehan discussed the idea of the four options all human beings have when in distress (2005):

1. Problem solve the situation.

2. Change your interpretation of the situation or how you feel about it.

3. Do nothing different and stay just as miserable as you are now.

4. Accept what you cannot change and go back to problem solving what you can change.

Sharon is distressed because she and a friend are both engaged, and every time they discuss their wedding ideas, Sharon feels her friend steals her ideas. What can Sharon do with this distress?

1. She can problem solve the situation by using her interpersonal effectiveness skills (see chapter 8).

2. As she uses emotion regulations skills, she can change her interpretation of this situation by focusing on how flattering it is that her friend loves all her ideas instead of focusing on her feelings that her friend is stealing her ideas (see chapter 6).

3. She can do nothing different, feeling bad about the friendship and using her bulimia to help her cope with how angry and helpless she feels. She will continue to feel miserable but will focus on feeling worse about herself after using behaviors instead of focusing on how hurt and angry she feels toward her friend.

4. She can accept that she cannot change who her friend is (especially if her interpersonal effectiveness skills don't get the desired response), and she can use distress tolerance skills to help her accept what she cannot change. Then Sharon will be thinking in a wiser, more balanced way, and then she can more effectively problem solve what she *can* change (how much she talks to her friend) and her interpretations (that her friend admires her).

In this chapter you will learn many skills and techniques to help you as you work toward creating a life worth being present in. Remember that using your bulimic behaviors might help you tolerate distress in the immediate moment (by checking out), but it almost always makes things worse for you in the long run. That is why you're reading this book. In this chapter you'll learn other ways to tolerate the distress in any given moment without making your life worse and without creating more problems that you then want to escape from by again using your bulimic behaviors. It's time to learn how to stop the cycle.

DISTRESS TOLERANCE SKILLS

As we discussed in chapter 6, throughout life you will have the experience of pain. Whether it is physical or emotional, pain is a part of life. Pain can be expected and can be partly within your control, like getting a shot at the doctor's office or having a significant other break up with you because you cheated. At other times, however, pain can be unpredictable and unavoidable, like the pain of someone accidentally stepping on your foot in line at the grocery store or the pain of feeling rejected when you have a crush on someone and they don't share your interest. Regardless of how the pain comes about, often the only way to help yourself is to use the coping skills you have and hope that they don't make your life worse. In this section you will learn coping skills that won't make your life worse and that you can use when pain comes suddenly and you can do nothing to change it in the moment.

Distract Yourself

In this section, you will learn ways to distract yourself from what is distressing you when you know that you can't do anything about it in the present moment.

Annie began treatment stating that she has been in and out of therapy for many years. She went on to explain that, while she had learned many contributing factors to the development of her bulimia and understood that it was mentally and physically very dangerous to her, she continued to use these behaviors and didn't know how to stop. When we described DBT, Annie commented that she hadn't ever learned what to do instead of using her bulimic behaviors. She described feeling that once she was in distress, there were no other options than to use these unhealthy and self-destructive behaviors to help her cope.

As we mentioned before, there are times when you might be in distress about a situation, but in the present moment you can do nothing to work on (problem solve or change your interpretation of) the situation. What *can* you do? If you're using your bulimic behaviors, then you are likely trying to escape certain feelings in a manner that only brings back more negative feelings for you to try to escape. Distraction can be a healthy and effective way to deal with a distressing situation that you can't change in the moment (Linehan 1993b).

When Carrie's boyfriend said he was going to call at 6:00 PM and he didn't, by 8:00 PM Carrie was ready to use bulimic behaviors to help her block her feelings of hurt and anger. But then she realized she was in emotion mind and did a mindfulness exercise to try to bring her back to wise mind. She realized that she could use her interpersonal effectiveness skills to try to talk with her boyfriend, but he wasn't answering his phone. Therefore, she needed to use distress tolerance skills because she couldn't change the situation in that moment. She just had to tolerate the feelings without making her life worse by using her bulimic behaviors. She was able to effectively use distraction skills to cope.

Be the BOSS of Distraction

In this section you're going to learn how to be the "BOSS" of distraction. Linehan notes that there are many different ways to distract oneself when in distress (1993b). She teaches how to distract with activities, contributing to others, comparisons, generating opposite emotions, pushing away from the situation, distracting with thoughts, and using strong sensations for distraction. Some of these ideas are referred to below.

B: FOCUS ON BEING BUSY

One way to distract yourself from a distressing situation that you cannot change in the moment is to focus on activities and being busy. There are many ways a person can be busy and remain actively distracted. Because you have an eating disorder, it might not be effective to use exercise as a healthy distraction from distress, as you could have the inclination to overuse exercise to an unhealthy degree. That's why exercise is not formally included here. If you are able to exercise without pressure or pain, then you might consider including taking a walk or participating in a team sport as an additional way to be busy with distraction.

Distracting Activities

Here's a list of some other things you can do to keep yourself distracted and focused on something you can get fully engaged in. Mark which activities might work for you:

Hobbies

_____ Music (listening to or creating)

_____ Playing computer games

_____ Writing

_____ Other _____

Arts and crafts

_____ Pottery

_____ Drawing or coloring

_____ Beading jewelry

_____ Knitting or weaving

_____ Other _____

Chores around the house

_____ Doing the dishes

_____ Cleaning or organizing your closets

_____ Gardening or mowing the lawn

_____ Other _____

O: FOCUS ONLY ON OTHERS

Another way to distract yourself from a distressing focus on a painful situation is to focus on others instead of yourself. Irene spoke about how she was angry with her husband after an argument one night. He went to bed without resolving the fight because he had to be at work very early the next day. Alone and still spinning from the argument, Irene knew she had to use distress tolerance skills to tolerate the situation without making it worse before she and her husband would have the opportunity to discuss it the next day. She decided to make his lunch that night as a way of focusing on him. Not only did her husband appreciate it, but Irene also had more positive feelings toward her husband when she was done.

Activities to Focus on Another

Here's a list of some things you can do to keep yourself distracted and focused on someone else so that your attention is off of yourself. Mark which activities might work for you:

Focus on people you love and feel loved by

_____ Call a friend

_____ Call a close family member

_____ Write a letter or e-mail to someone far away

_____ Other _____

Focus on doing something nice for someone else by volunteering to help others

_____ In a soup kitchen

_____ In a hospital

_____ In a youth group

_____ In an eating disorders advocacy group

_____ Other _____

Focus on nice things others have done for you

_____ Helped you (clean, pack and move, run an errand)

_____ Checked on you when you weren't feeling well

_____ Gave you gifts

_____ Other _____

Focus on how other people are doing in comparison to you

_____ Focus on others who are coping as well as or worse than you

_____ Focus on how others' situations might be worse than yours (even on TV shows or in the news)

_____ Other _____

S: FOCUS ON STRONG SENSATIONS

Another way to distract yourself from a distressing situation that you cannot change in the moment is to focus on strong sensations. Because you have an eating disorder, it wouldn't be effective to use your sense of taste as a healthy distraction from distress. In fact, that's probably how the bulimia currently functions, to some degree.

Focusing on Strong Sensations

Here's a list of some things you can do to keep yourself distracted with strong sensations. Mark which activities might work for you:

Focus on intense sight

_____ Look at some artwork by M. C. Escher and try to figure it out

_____ Do a mindfulness exercise of observing a flame

_____ Other _____

Focus on intense sound

_____ Listen to loud music

_____ Do a mindfulness exercise of listening to one piece of music several times, each time focusing on a different instrument

_____ Other _____

Focus on intense scents

_____ Smelling salts

_____ Incense or potpourri

_____ Other _____

Focus on intense touch

_____ Holding ice cubes in your hands

_____ Taking a very hot or very cold shower

_____ Other _____

S: FOCUS ON STATEMENTS OF SELF-SUPPORT

A final way to distract yourself from focusing on a distressing situation that you cannot change in the moment is to focus on statements of self-support.

Distracting with Supportive Statements

Here's a list of some things you can do to keep yourself distracted and focused on supportive statements. Mark which activities might work for you:

Focus on encouraging statements

_____ "I can tolerate this experience even though I don't like it."

_____ Do a mindfulness exercise of focusing on your breath. On the in breath, say to yourself, "Just this one...," and on the out breath say to yourself, "...moment." This will help you focus on the idea that *anything* can be tolerated in just one moment, and life is just a series of moments strung together.

_____ "I am doing as well as I can given all that has led up to this point."

_____ "Focusing on the past and future only prevents me from living in the present."

_____ Other _____

Focus on acknowledging your current vulnerabilities

_____ "I'm tired because I didn't get enough sleep, and won't feel this bad when I'm better rested."

_____ "I haven't eaten for four to five hours, and therefore I'm hungry and unfocused. I'll feel better when I've eaten healthfully."

_____ Other _____

Focus on acceptance statements

_____ "Everything is as it should be."

_____ "I cannot control others or their reactions."

_____ "I cannot change this in this moment, and I can tolerate it."

_____ Other _____

As you might have noticed, Ed mind can actually function as a form of distraction as you focus on body image and food to prevent you from thinking about all of the potentially stressful things in your life. This is why focusing on taste isn't listed as an effective focus for distraction with sensations.

When you can do nothing about a distressing situation, distraction is effective. However, if you use it when you can do something to problem solve or change your interpretation of the situation, then distraction is no longer effective because it prevents you from dealing with the present moment. Using bulimia to cope becomes addictive because, as you use it to cope, it causes more problems that you have to then cope with (relationship problems, productivity problems at work or school, self-esteem problems, and so on). Then you turn to these behaviors even when you could be problem solving, changing your interpretation, or accepting the situation. Distraction can be overused even with healthy forms of distraction, such as those we offered above. It is always more effective to problem solve or change your interpretation of a situation if change is possible. However, when you truly can't do anything to change the facts of the situation, distraction can be useful. For instance, when Tony was waiting to hear about whether he passed his medical school boards, he couldn't problem solve the situation, and he couldn't change his interpretation of the meaning (importance) of the test. He had to accept that he couldn't change the reality of his situation—he had to wait four to six weeks to hear the results. So he used his mindfulness skills to notice when thoughts about the test popped unintentionally into his mind, and then he used distraction skills to tolerate the ensuing distress.

Learning to Soothe Yourself

Once you've learned to use mindfulness to be aware in the present moment and to be self-aware, you might begin to feel that you don't have the tools to deal with that awareness. There's a point in the movie *The Matrix* where the main character, Neo, is asked if he wants to take a blue pill or a red pill. The blue pill will take Neo back to the life he had been living: unaware of reality and living only in the perceptions of his mind. The red pill will help awaken him to the truth of his situation, and once he's awakened, he cannot leave that truth behind. Mindfulness is like taking the red pill. You learn to be really present in your life instead of in your head. One important note is that truth is sometimes painful, and when you see the truth, you need to have the skills to tolerate the occasional pain that inevitably comes with it. You've learned the skills of distraction, but they can only be effective for so long. Now you'll learn about how you can soothe yourself when feeling distressed. Linehan refers to soothing oneself with the five senses, which can be very effective (1993b). It is often said that babies need to learn to soothe themselves to sleep or they end up depending on their parents to get them to sleep every night. If a baby never learns how to soothe himself, he will always be dependent on his parents for soothing, whether in bed, at school, or on the playground. When a child doesn't learn healthy soothing techniques, he often develops harmful coping strategies. After all, parents can't always be there to soothe, and if you haven't learned healthy ways to soothe yourself, you may turn to things like bingeing, drugs, alcohol, cutting, purging, or gambling as ultimately ineffective methods of self-soothing. Let's look at some healthy self-soothing skills that use your five senses.

SOOTHING WITH SIGHT

A large portion of the human brain is devoted solely to sight (the occipital lobe). Many people are visual thinkers and even imagine pictures when they read a story. When soothing with the sense of sight, you'll focus on visual objects that bring you comfort and relaxation. For example, Carrie would work with brightly colored beads when distressed because she found it soothing to look at the rainbow of colors in the beads and felt calm as she put the colorful beads together to make beautiful jewelry.

Visual Activities

Here are some possible sight activities that you can do to soothe yourself. Remember that not all activities will work for everyone, so give different ones a try to see what might work for you. Mark the ones that worked:

_____ Use a camera to help you focus (through the lens) on nature.

_____ Do a mindfulness exercise of observing a picture. Notice when your mind tries to describe the picture and nonjudgmentally bring your attention back to observing what you see.

_____ Have some flowers in a few rooms in your home so that you see them as you walk around. You can also choose to sit and focus on them.

_____ Other _____

SOOTHING WITH SOUND

Sound has long been associated with the ability to soothe. The poetic line "Music has charms to soothe a savage breast" is quite telling. Parents soothe their babies by softly singing or humming a lullaby.

Even Frankenstein's monster was soothed with the sound of a violin. Using sound can work as a very effective self-soothing skill. When soothing with the sense of sound, you focus on listening to sounds in the room that can bring you comfort and relaxation.

Sound Activities

Here are some possible sound activities that you can do to soothe yourself with sound. As with the visual activities, try different ones and do what works for you. Mark the activities that worked:

_____ Listen to soft, melodic music that doesn't make you sad.

_____ Do a mindfulness exercise of observing sound. Sit quietly in a room and simply open your ears to any sound that comes. Notice when your mind labels the sounds and bring your attention back with equanimity to observing what you hear without labeling or describing. Notice when your mind wanders to other thoughts and bring your attention back to observing what you hear without labeling or describing.

_____ Listen to the sounds of nature (in nature, on a video, on a CD, or from a sound machine). For example, listen to the sounds of a beach, the shore of a lake, or a rainforest.

_____ Other _____

SOOTHING WITH SCENT

The sense of smell has a strong connection with memory. Have you ever noticed that you can catch a certain scent and it seems to transport you back to a time when you had an experience with that fragrance? When Ellie smells chlorine, she thinks about swimming during the summers of her childhood. When she smells the perfume Chanel No. 5, she thinks about her high school friend who would wear that perfume. Smell can be an effective self-soothing sense, but again, we have to be careful of Ed's attempts to turn a healthful skill into a tool supporting your eating disorder. People often associate the sense of smell with the sense of taste. Again, we aren't using taste as a skill here because focusing on taste might make you feel more vulnerable to a binge. Many people with eating disorders say they don't even taste the food in a binge. In this case, learning to focus on and really notice smell and taste might eventually prove useful in slowing down or preventing a binge. However, because you're just getting started in using these skills, it's best to hold off on using taste until you've had a bit more experience.

Activities Using the Sense of Smell

Here are some possible activities that you can do to soothe with smell. Mark which activities might work for you:

_____ Try some new air fresheners. Pick one that's very soothing to you and spray it around your home.

_____ Do a mindfulness exercise of observing smells in nature. Go for a walk outside and breathe in through your nose, focusing your attention on what you smell. This can be a very different experience during different seasons of the year. Notice the scents in the air. Notice when your mind labels these fragrances and bring your attention back with equanimity to observing what you smell without labeling or describing.

_____ Light some lavender-scented candles and then sit quietly in the room.

_____ Other _____

SOOTHING WITH TOUCH

The sense of touch can have a powerful soothing effect. For example, Annie noticed her emotional vulnerabilities to distress and decided that instead of buying food to binge on, she would use her DBT skills. To soothe herself, she did a mindfulness exercise of focusing on the touch of her soft scarf. She was able to feel better and return to work without using bulimic behaviors. Touch can be an effective self-soothing sense. In the 1950s, experiments conducted by psychologist Harry Harlow on maternal deprivation in rhesus monkeys showed that when the baby monkeys were frightened by strange, loud objects, the ones with access to terry-cloth-covered "surrogate mothers" rubbed against them to help them calm down (Harlow 1958). Likewise, young children often like their backs rubbed as they try to fall asleep.

Activities Using Touch

Here are some possible activities that you can do to soothe with the sense of touch. Mark which activities might work for you:

_____ Pet a loved animal or go to a pet store and play with a puppy or a kitten for a while.

_____ Take a warm shower or a bath with soothing bubbles, bath beads, or bath salts.

_____ Do a mindfulness exercise of observing the feeling of something soft (silk, chenille, velvet, a stuffed animal). Notice the feeling of the object on your fingers and hands. Observe when your mind labels what you are touching and bring your attention back with equanimity to noticing the experience on your fingers and hands without labeling or describing.

_____ Other _____

Creating a Self-Soothing Kit

Now that you have learned some ways to soothe yourself with your senses, make a list that you can keep in your wallet or your purse so that you can remember these skills when you are in distress. Like Annie, who was away from home when in distress, you need to be prepared with soothing tools readily available. Have a soothing kit in your bedroom, in your car, at your desk, or wherever appropriate. Try to have one or two tools for each sense. For example, you might have a camera or a special photograph in your soothing kit. You can have a soothing CD to play in your car or a sound machine in your bedroom. In your kit you might also have a few perfume samples or a fragrant candle, as well as a soft scarf and favorite small stuffed animal. Then you can use these sensory distraction skills as soon as you become mindful that you need them or aware that you are in distress.

Tolerating Distress by Finding Another Focus in the Moment

When humans are in distress, it's most natural for us to focus on the negatives of the situation. While distraction can be an effective way to tolerate distress, another way is to find another, more positive focus (Linehan 1993b). Linehan suggests that people "improve the moment" by using techniques or redirecting their focus. The following skills can allow you to feel more empowered as you face distress because you can determine what you focus on and decide which focus works most effectively for you.

FIND YOUR HAPPY PLACE

When stressed-out, you can choose to find an imagined happy place or safe place to go to. What this means is that you imagine a place, using all of your senses, that you can visit in your mind when in distress. To do this, you need to first think about what type of place would be most relaxing for you.

Creating Your Happy Place

Answer the following questions to help define your happy place.

Are you indoors or outside?

_____

Are you in a closed-off room or is there fresh air?

_____

Is the temperature hot, warm, cool, or cold?

_____

Is there someone or something (like a pet) there with you?

_____

What do you hear?

_____

What do you see?

_____

What do you smell?

_____

What do you feel?

_____

One example might be to imagine sitting on a beach with the sun warming your skin while a gentle, cool breeze blows. You might hear the waves crashing and the seagulls flying overhead. You might imagine seeing the clouds floating by as you watch the waves lap up on the shore, and you can almost taste the salt air when you open your mouth to breathe. You can imagine the feeling of the warm sand underneath your hands and your feet. Tune in to all of your senses when you go to this place.

FIND A HIGHER POWER

Whether or not you practice a formal religion, you can connect to a higher power. Your higher power does not have to be God. For example, when Ellie sees a peaceful, colorful sunset, she describes feeling in touch with a spiritual place inside of her. You can connect to this sense of a higher power by being aware that there are things bigger than us all in life.

FIND ONE FOCUS

In the moments when you're very distressed, it can be effective to put all of your attention on only one thing. You've probably had the experience of feeling distressed about one thing, then you mind jumps to another distressing thought or situation, and another on top of that. When you're anxious, angry, sad, and so on, your mind is likely to skip from one problem to another, compounding the distress you're feeling. The next thing you know, you're feeling overwhelmed as your mind races with all that you have to do, all that you have done, regrets, and fears. Part of why you feel overwhelmed is because you're focusing on a million things at once, and your mind can't do that comfortably. When you become aware that your mind is racing this way, you can choose to focus on only one thing to recenter you thoughts. Focus on just what you're doing in that moment. For example, if you're driving and running late for work, you might find your mind jumping ahead to all the things you need to do and prepare for once you get to work, making you feel even worse. When this happens, focus all of your attention only on the task of driving. What are your legs doing? What are your arms and hands doing? What do you have to focus your eyes on to drive safely? Notice all of the physical sensations and the voluntary movements necessary to do what you're doing in that moment. Work will be there when you get there, and if you can get yourself to a mindful, soothed place before you arrive, you'll function more effectively.

FIND A PURPOSE

When you're in distress, it can help to find a purpose for your painful feelings. In other words, you can look for the opportunity behind what you see as a misfortune. For example, when Ellie was distressed about her knee injury and the accompanying knee brace she had to wear, she was able to observe her distress and take some distance. From that distance, she was able to find a purpose to her knee injury—she could use this distress to practice her distress tolerance skills. Though it was no fun to be stuck in a knee brace, Ellie chose to look at it as an opportunity to get better at a skill that she valued.

FIND RELAXATION

It's nearly impossible to feel distressed when your body is relaxed. So you can use relaxation techniques to help you feel better in moments of pain. A great technique for relaxing is called progressive muscle relaxation. Here's how you do it.

Find a comfortable position in a quiet place. Pay attention to your breathing for a few moments. Now go through the muscle groups in your body one by one, starting with your hands. For a count of ten, clench your fists as tightly as you can. Focus on the tension of the feelings in your fingers, thumbs, and palms. After the count of ten, release your hands and let them relax. Notice the difference in the sensations in your hands.

Now move to your arms. For a count of ten, flex the muscles in your arms as tightly as you can. Focus on the feelings of tension in your lower and upper arms. After the count of ten, release your arms and let them relax. Notice the difference in the sensations in your arms.

Now move to your shoulders. For a count of ten, flex the muscles in your shoulders as tightly as you can. Focus on this tension in your shoulders and back. After the count of ten, release your shoulders and let them relax. Notice the difference in the sensations in your shoulders.

Now move to your head. For a count of ten, flex the muscles in your head and face as tightly as you can. Focus on the feelings of tension in the back of your head, your forehead, your jaws, and your face. After the count of ten, release the muscles in your head and face and let them relax. Notice the difference in the sensations in your head and face.

Now move to your stomach. For a count of ten, flex the muscles in your stomach as tightly as you can. Focus on this tension in your stomach and back. After the count of ten, release your stomach muscles and let them relax. Notice the difference in the sensations in your stomach.

Now you can move through the rest of your muscle groups in your body, doing the same thing. Do this with your bottom, your thighs, your calves, and your feet. This exercise will aid your muscles to recall what a state of relaxation feels like, and therefore it will help you to find relaxation.

FIND SELF-ENCOURAGING STATEMENTS

You probably aren't used to thinking of encouraging statements for yourself but are very familiar with self-discouraging statements. The skill of using self-encouraging statements is similar to the earlier skill that focused on statements of self-support. Earlier we talked about distracting with encouraging statements, statements acknowledging vulnerabilities, and statements of acceptance. In this section, the self-encouraging statements aren't meant to be used as a distraction; rather, use them as encouragement not to give up on using your skills while acknowledging the urge to do so. Take this opportunity to write down some self-encouraging statements that you can use when you are in distress. Here are some examples:

- "I can choose to do something different instead of using my bulimia and staying miserable."

- "Even when I feel like I can't keep fighting the urge, I can notice the thoughts urging me to give up, and I can use my distress tolerance skills to keep going and to redirect my attention."

- "Ed used to help, but turning to Ed doesn't make my life better."

- "I can accept the joy in life *and* tolerate the pain."

- "I want to and I can be present in my life."

Now you think of a few and write them here:

_____

_____

_____

_____

Now that you've learned how to tolerate distress by finding another focus in the moment, you can find your happy place, find a higher power, find one focus in the moment, find a purpose, find relaxation, and find self-encouraging statements to help you through distress without making things worse in your life.

Tolerating Distress by Focusing on Values

The word "value" has many definitions. The definition that most applies here is "something (as a principle or quality) intrinsically valuable or desirable." When people think of values, they think of morals, ethics, and ideals. Do you know what the values are that matter to you most? How do you think your healthy values might differ from your Ed values? How do you figure out your values? When considering what you truly value, it's important to be aware of certain judgments that can creep into this decision. Would you rate certain values more highly if you didn't judge them? One person might find experiencing pleasure in life (playtime) as a high personal value, while another person may judge play as not especially valuable. Georgia was a call girl many years ago, and then shebegan to work in a more socially acceptable business. During a financial crisis, she lost everything, and she again contacted a couple of old clients. She described feeling bad about herself for returning to sex work, and she used her bulimia after every visit with a client. However, one of her core personal values was financial success, so she felt compelled to do what it took to be financially comfortable. As her treatment progressed, she could pull back from judging her priorities while she reprioritized the values that supported healthy behaviors in her life. Gradually, these healthy values took priority over financial success. She was then able to stop seeing her clients, felt better about herself, and could use her skills more effectively.

Assessing Your Values

Everyone has their own values for a variety of reasons. To begin sorting out what you truly value, take a look at thirteen items commonly referred to as values:

- Appearance
- Financial success
- Having others like you
- Health
- Playtime
- Relaxation time
- Wisdom

- Being loyal and trustworthy
- Hard work
- Having others respect you
- Meaningful relationships
- Power
- Spirituality

Choose the three that are most important to you and rank them below.

1. _____

2. _____

3. _____

How much time and energy do you devote to your top three values?

_____

_____

_____

_____

Differentiating Your Values

Now that you've begun to think about and rate your values in importance, you're ready to differentiate your positive, healthy values from Ed's values, which likely aren't so effective for you. To start with, take a look at the complete list of values and, in the left column, rank them (from 1 to 13) according to which values are most important to *you* (meaning the part of you that thinks in a wise and balanced way). Those with lower numbers are the values you wish you devoted the most time and energy to, even if they aren't currently the values that you work the hardest on.

	You	Ed
Appearance	_____	_____
Being loyal and trustworthy	_____	_____
Financial success	_____	_____
Hard work	_____	_____
Having others like you	_____	_____
Having others respect you	_____	_____
Health	_____	_____
Meaningful relationships	_____	_____
Playtime	_____	_____
Power	_____	_____
Relaxation time	_____	_____
Spirituality	_____	_____
Wisdom	_____	_____

Now go back through the list and rate Ed's values.

How do the two sets of rankings match up? Where do they differ?

_____

_____

Now, whenever you find yourself in Ed mind, you can go back through this list of values to help you recall how they differ and how working toward your own true values will help you live a life that you want to be present in. This will help you be mindful of the fact that Ed's values will only take you down a path of wanting to escape the chaos that Ed creates. By turning to Ed more, you will lose the things that are really important to you—the people and things that involve your wise-minded values.

Fulfilling Your True Values

Now that you're able to distinguish your wise-minded values from your Ed-minded values, it's time to start thinking about how to fulfill the values that are healthy for you. Think about two steps that you can do toward fulfilling your wise-minded values. For example, if one of your top values is health, you might consider a plan with the goals to quit smoking or to get to bed a bit earlier.

Wise-minded value 1: _____

    Step 1: _____

    Step 2: _____

Wise-minded value 2: _____

    Step 1: _____

    Step 2: _____

Wise-minded value 3: _____

    Step 1: _____

    Step 2: _____

As you do this exercise, make sure you're writing down realistic, doable steps to help you create a plan that you can actually execute. If one step looks too big upon reflection, then break that step down into smaller steps. For example, if going to bed earlier looks like an unrealistic goal, you can break your evening down into steps. Then you can begin to figure out where you can cut back on your evening routine to make going to bed earlier more realistic. Remember that the purpose of this exercise is to help you create a life in which you want to be present.

Tolerating Distress by Being Present in the Moment

Another way to tolerate distress is to keep your focus in the present moment. This is a similar idea to what we talked about in the example of driving to work late. When we discussed finding one focus, we were suggesting that you find anything to focus on as long as you put all of your attention toward that one thing. This skill, being present in the moment, helps you tolerate distress by turning all of your attention to what is happening in the present moment—right now. Focusing on being present *in this moment* can help you tolerate distress by focusing all of your attention on your total sensorial experience of this one moment. People often intensify and prolong distress because they think about their regrets and anxieties about the past and their fears and lack of control over the future. It can be very helpful to notice when you're focused on the past and the future. When you notice this happening, you can choose to redirect your attention so that you can focus on the present moment.

From a practical standpoint, how do you focus on the present moment? When Sara was getting married, a close friend suggested that sometime during the wedding she take a few minutes and "just take it all in." She later described those moments as amazing, as she observed, with all of her senses, everything that was going on around her and everything that was going on inside of her. Years later, she hasn't forgotten that experience of being truly present at her wedding.

Describing Your Present Moment

To describe your present moment, become mindful of all that is around you and all that is inside of you. Use the following questions to help you expand your awareness of the present moment.

Where are you right now? Are you inside or outside? Are you at home or somewhere else?

_____

_____

_____

What are you doing? Are you resting? Are you doing an activity?

_____

_____

_____

What are you thinking about? Are you focused on a regret about the past? Are you worrying about something you can't control in the future?

_____

_____

_____

What's going on with you physically? Are you feeling tension or tightness anywhere in your body? Are you tired? Are you hot or cold?

_____

_____

_____

What are your senses telling you? What do you hear? What is the taste in your mouth? If your fingers are touching something, what does that surface feel like? What do you smell? What do you see?

_____

_____

_____

As you do this exercise, try to use your skills of observation without judgment. The objective is to simply notice mindfully, through your senses, this present moment. When you're fully in the moment, you can't be focused on distress about the past or future.

RADICAL ACCEPTANCE

Now that you've learned how to tolerate distress when you can't change things in the moment, through distraction and redirecting your focus, it's crucial that you learn about *radical acceptance* (Linehan 1993b). What is radical acceptance and how can it help with bulimia? One definition of radical is "drastic or sweeping; extreme," and one for acceptance is "belief in something or agreement." So radical acceptance is a drastic or extreme belief in something. Another way to understand it is to view radical acceptance as a deep recognition of and lack of struggle with the reality of your situation. This does *not* imply that you approve of whatever it is that you need to accept. It doesn't even mean that you like the reality that you're trying to accept. It simply means that you believe the reality down to your core, in your wise mind, and without judgment, and that you give up struggling with how things really are. This type of acceptance can be very unfamiliar, because people tend to think that if they don't like something, they shouldn't accept it. To many, accepting the reality of a situation equates with liking or approving of it. The reality is that not liking something and not accepting it doesn't make it change. Not accepting something that you don't like works to keep you stuck in an overly emotional state of mind and keeps you being miserable—because if you can't accept a reality, you can't begin to strategize about how to cope with it or change it.

Your Options When in Distress

To further understand the four options available to you when you're feeling distressed and how to implement them, try this exercise. Think of one example of a situation in your life that is currently making you feel distress.

What can you do to problem solve the situation?

_____

_____

What interpretation are you currently making?

_____

_____

Write down a new possible interpretation.

_____

_____

What would you do if you were going to cope as you typically do? If you do that, how miserable will you be on a scale of 1 to 10 (1 being not at all miserable and 10 being the most miserable you have ever felt)?

_____

_____

How miserable would you be if you coped more effectively without using your typical bulimic behaviors? How miserable will you be on a scale of 1 to 10 (1 being not at all miserable and 10 being the most miserable you have ever felt)?

_____

Even though you might not like it, what do you know you cannot change about the situation (for example, you cannot change other people)? What do you have to radically accept?

_____

_____

Now that you're clear on what you cannot change, what *can* you change?

_____

_____

After doing this exercise, you might be thinking, "That's all fine and dandy, but how do I get myself to accept things that I cannot change?" Remember that pain without acceptance leads to misery—to suffering. Pain *with* acceptance is simply pain. It's an experience that can be tolerated even when we doubt that we can cope. Pain ebbs and flows in life, and a lack of acceptance intensifies the experience by making you focus on the pain so that it feels more intense and lasts longer. To radically accept what you cannot change means to choose to use the skills in this chapter, over and over again, even when your emotions tell you to give up.

You might think that you already accept reality in most instances. However, consider the last time you asked yourself why something was happening or how that thing could be happening to you. Those questions are indicative of lack of acceptance. People with bulimia often ask, "Why do I have bulimia?"; "How could I have developed bulimia?"; or "Why can't I just stop?" Questions like these are often entangled with tons of judgment. The reality is that you *do* have bulimia. That doesn't make you good or bad—it is what it is. If you don't accept that reality, you'll spend a lot of time and energy trying to figure these things out or trying to deny the reality, rather than figuring out how to stop the behaviors. However, if you can radically accept that you have bulimia, then you can spend that time and energy working toward problem solving about tolerating the reality and effectively dealing with it. This is a core notion in DBT: balancing acceptance and change (Linehan 1993b). You need to accept where you are and what you cannot change while working toward changing what you can.

You likely struggle with accepting reality on all kinds of levels, from not wanting to accept the reality that a friend is busy and can't go out with you to not wanting to accept the death of a loved one. For instance, Mariah didn't want to accept that her boyfriend had broken up with her and all that the fact meant in her life. She continually questioned, "Why? What could I have done differently to prevent this? And how do I get him to change his mind?" She wasn't accepting the reality that she couldn't control her ex or his feelings—that all she can control is herself. She was experiencing great suffering by not accepting the reality of the pain, and therefore she was miserable. Mariah had to work toward radical acceptance to be able to decrease her misery. She had to radically accept the breakup and accept that she couldn't change the reality of her situation. With some effort, she was eventually able to radically accept this reality using her DBT skills more effectively. Her skills helped her to ride the waves of emotion and redirect her attention when she focused on questions that perpetuated her lack of acceptance. She was able to act opposite to her urges of love by avoiding her ex-boyfriend and not pursuing contact. She was able to recognize that thinking and rethinking the past and the relationship was futile. She would never know the answers to these questions unless she asked her ex, and she had no intention of asking him. She came to accept that even if she knew those answers, they wouldn't change her reality in the present. Mariah used her distress-tolerance skills to help distract herself when she focused on the former relationship because she realized that this focus simply kept her miserable. She made more of an effort to experience positive emotions (using techniques from chapter 6) so that she had less time to focus on negatives. Mariah was able to decrease her misery by using her DBT skills effectively to tolerate her pain and to reach radical acceptance.

Reaching Radical Acceptance

The next time you find yourself in a distressing situation, ask yourself the following questions as you work toward radical acceptance.

What is the situation?

_____

_____

How did you contribute to this situation?

_____

_____

Who else contributed to the situation and how?

_____

_____

Is this a situation that you can change or control?

_____

_____

Are the actions others who are involved something that you can change or control?

_____

_____

Is the end result something you can change or control?

_____

_____

If you don't accept the situation, how will you feel?

_____

_____

If you accept the situation, how will things be different?

_____

_____

To gain a more in-depth understanding of how radical acceptance can help, let's take a look at Ellie's experience. Ellie was on vacation with her husband in Florida. They were waiting to get into Epcot, and her husband mentioned that his band was due to go on the road in three weeks. Ellie felt alarmed and reminded him that they had scheduled a big family function in three weeks. Her husband replied that he couldn't cancel the band's gig because that would hurt the band's reputation with the managers at this location. Ellie responded by immediately entering emotion mind. She was hurt because she felt her husband was putting the band before their family and angry that he hadn't remembered their family commitments when he scheduled the gig.

After taking a mindful moment and realizing that she didn't want her whole day ruined by being in emotion mind, Ellie thought about the questions in the previous exercise. She realized that she had contributed to the situation she was experiencing in that moment by mentioning that the family function was already booked. Her husband contributed because he had made an assumption that the family function was on a Sunday (because they usually were) and didn't check out the facts. Ellie realized that she couldn't change the situation because the gig was already scheduled and her husband was unwilling to cancel it. She was aware that she couldn't change or control her husband's decision about this, and therefore she couldn't control the end result. Ellie recognized that if she couldn't change or problem solve the situation in the moment and yet remained unwilling to accept the situation and her lack of control, she would likely feel miserable and angry all day. She knew that if she accepted what she couldn't change, then she would be able to enjoy the rest of the day and think about problem solving when she had some distance from it. By the end of a really nice day, she and her husband were able to discuss the situation. Her husband apologized for his role in the problem and explained that they had cancelled on this location once before (he didn't tell her that initially because he was feeling so defensive). He agreed to try to reschedule the gig, and she agreed that if he couldn't reschedule, then she would radically accept his absence at the family function. He assured her that he didn't want to miss the family function, and that he would really feel like he was missing out. They also engaged in some problem solving about how to avoid this issue in the future.

Radical Acceptance Isn't the End

All the skills you've learned in this chapter (and in the rest of the book) will help you to reach radical acceptance. But it's imperative to recognize that radical acceptance isn't the end of the line. It's not as though you radically accept something and everything is unchangingly fine. Radical acceptance is something that you must choose to work toward over and over again. It's likely that even when you radically accept problems, you'll still feel hopeless at times and not want to use skills. You may radically accept that you have bulimia. You may radically accept that using DBT skills will help you live a life worth being present in. You may radically accept that bulimia actually helps you check out of life. Even after you have accepted all of these realities, you will still have times when you just don't want to use your skills or feel hopeless about whether the skills will help. This is when you will need to choose again to work toward radical acceptance. Realities don't remain static; feelings and situations are bound to change. Because of the ever-changing nature of life, radical acceptance is a skill that everyone needs to use over and over again.

CONCLUSION

In this chapter you've learned about the common human experience of distress and pain. You learned new coping skills for use in tolerating feelings you've typically tried to avoid by turning to your bulimia. You now know about the four options that any human being has in any distressing situation: you can problem solve the situation, change your interpretation of the situation, do nothing different and stay just as miserable as you are now, or you can radically accept what you cannot change and go back to problem solving what you *can* change it. If you can't problem solve or change the interpretation (as is often the case with distressing situations), then you can either do nothing and stay miserable or you can use distress tolerance techniques to work toward radical acceptance. If you choose to work toward radical acceptance, you've learned skills that can help in this quest. You know the effectiveness of distracting yourself when you cannot change a distressing situation. Bear in mind, however, that distraction carries the risk of being overused because people sometimes choose to distract when it would be much more effective to problem solve or change your interpretation of the situation. You have also learned how to soothe yourself by focusing on four main senses (sight, hearing, scent, and touch). You now understand how to tolerate distress by finding another focus in the moment and by focusing on your wise-minded values. Because you've learned to be present in and keep your focus on the present moment, you are now better able to tolerate events in the moment. All of these skills have the enabled you to work toward radical acceptance and find your way into a life worth living.

CHAPTER 8

Interpersonal Skills

So far, you've become familiar with a number of important skills: mindfulness, emotion regulation, and distress tolerance. We hope you've been practicing and will continue to practice these skills, as they work in tandem to help you build a life worth being present in. In this chapter, we will go over skills to use in relationships. Skills for interpersonal effectiveness can help you repair, maintain, and improve your relationships with friends, coworkers, partners, spouses, family members, and virtually anyone you might interact with. These skills can help you solve problems before they get big or even head them off before they start. They can also help you end relationships that are painful and cannot be improved.

WHY WORKING ON RELATIONSHIPS IS IMPORTANT

You might wonder why we include a chapter on interpersonal skills in a workbook on bulimia. For some people, the connection between relationships and their eating problems are clear. For others, it may be a bit elusive. As therapists, it has been our experience that there often is a very important association between problems in relationships and bulimia. The patterns linking bulimia to relationship problems, like many others we have discussed so far, often turn out to be variations on the vicious circle.

For example, Donna would often severely restrict her food intake for several days at a time and then binge. Her bingeing behavior would be very obvious to her husband, who would get quite concerned about her. Out of his concern, he would start to criticize her, hoping to get her to stop. His criticism would lead to an increase in her stress and her own self-criticism. As her stress and self-criticism increased, she would start to restrict, initiating the whole chain of behaviors again. After understanding this pattern, Donna was able to use skills at many points along the chain to soothe herself and break the cycle. In particular, she started using interpersonal skills to make it clear to her husband that she understood his concern and that he really wanted to be helpful to her. She was able to explain that the way he was trying to help her actually made the problem worse, and that he could be more helpful by being more emotionally supportive of her and encouraging. While she needed to repeat this request a number of times, and also use other interpersonal skills, her husband gradually learned to reduce his criticism and be a more supportive partner to her.

In the following sections we will cover a range of interpersonal skills. We will help you learn how to identify and balance your needs with what others expect of you (Linehan 1993b) and your own wants with your obligations (Marlatt and Gordon 1985). Finding these balances will help you reduce your stress and achieve more effective levels of involvement in life. We will teach you a way of thinking about interactions that can aid you in figuring out your goals. You will also gain an understanding about what things might get in the way of your ability to be effective interpersonally, and we'll offer some suggestions for how to address them. Finally, we will cover skills for helping you get more of what you want and need while you maintain or improve your relationships and work to increase your self-respect.

Of course, as with all of the skills in this book, interpersonal skills can be difficult to put into practice. If having good relationships was easy, there wouldn't be so many self-help books on the market about improving them or getting out of them when they're bad. So we recommend that you practice these skills over and over. Remember that change often happens slowly. Be persistent!

IMPROVING BALANCE IN YOUR LIFE

When important elements in your life are out of balance, the result can be stressful, depressing, or overwhelming and may lead to a life that feels empty or valueless. Finding balance can lead to increased feelings of fulfillment, richness, and reward. For example, Ellie found that she alternated between feeling overwhelmed for days straight and then empty for long periods of time. When she began to understand how she acted on what was important to her and what was important to other people, her patterns of behavior became clear. She noted that she would spend many days at a time responding almost exclusively to other people's expectations and requests of her. At work, she would spend much of her time responding to coworkers' requests for help and her supervisor's demands for assistance. In her personal life, she noticed that she would pay a lot of attention to friends who needed support or just someone to listen to them. During these periods when she was attending to others, she would seldom if ever pay attention to what she needed: her own day-to-day tasks at work, her housework, or her desire for enjoyment or relaxation. As a consequence, Ellie would feel overwhelmed and irritable. She realized that when these feelings peaked, she had a tendency to pull back from others. She stopped paying attention to coworkers, avoided her supervisor, and stopped answering phone calls from friends. During the times she pulled back, she had more time to herself, could relax more, and had time to get her own work done. Pulling back helped her stop feeling overwhelmed and irritable; but the longer she stayed in this pattern of behavior, the more her life seemed empty and without value. She also saw how pulling back like this led to other problems on the job and in her friendships. Her friends and coworkers couldn't understand what her withdrawal meant, and tension would build with her supervisor. She also saw that her likelihood of engaging in bulimic behaviors increased both during the times she felt overwhelmed and when she felt empty. Once Ellie understood these patterns, she found she was better able to stay aware of the balance she needed in her life. She used the skills you'll learn later in this chapter to negotiate balance in her relationships. She experienced fewer swings in her emotions, felt more fulfilled, and found it easier to stop her bingeing and purging.

Balancing Your Needs and What Is Expected or Demanded of You

An important first step in achieving better balance in your life is identifying your needs, what others expect of you, your wants, and your obligations (Linehan 1993b; Marlatt and Gordon 1985; Gambrill and Richey 1985). Let's go over some definitions to make this clearer.

- **Your needs:** These are things that are very important for you to have, such as the need to feel safe in a relationship or the need to have adequate time to get important things done at work.

- **Others' expectations:** These are things that others want from you. Maybe your partner wants some space after work, or a friend expects you to be available when she's upset.

- **Your wants:** These are things that you want in your life because you enjoy them. Maybe you want to have time to read a good novel or hang out with friends.

- **Your obligations:** These are things that you tell yourself must be done. For example, you have an obligation to pay your bills and attend to household tasks.

While some things might fall into multiple categories (for instance, you might both need and have an obligation to pay your bills), often the things in each category are separate and distinct. An easy way of remembering these different factors is the acronym No Woe (needs, obligations, wants, and others' expectations).

Determining Your No Woe

The next step is to identify these important factors in each major area or relationship in your life. Use the following series of questions to help you do this. Start by figuring out these factors in your most important relationship. We'll give you ideas about other relationships where you might do this after you finish.

What are the things you need in this relationship?

_____

_____

_____

_____

What are the things that the other person in this relationship expects of you?

_____

_____

_____

_____

Now figure out whether your needs and the other person's expectations of you seem to be in balance. Do you regularly get what you need, or do you go without? Do you regularly grant the other person's expectations, or do you ignore or refuse them? If there seems to be balance, that's great. If things seem to be out of balance, how do you see this manifesting?

_____

_____

_____

_____

What are the things you want in this relationship?

_____

_____

_____

_____

What are the things you feel obligated to do in this relationship?

_____

_____

_____

_____

Now figure out whether your wants and obligations seem to be in balance. Do you regularly get what you want, or do you go without? Do you regularly take care of your obligations, or do you ignore or avoid them? If there seems to be balance, that's great. If things seem to be out of balance, describe how this shows up.

_____

_____

_____

_____

Now that you've finished this first exploration of these balances, you might want to repeat this process for other important relationships or areas of your life. Examples might include important friends, family members, supervisors, coworkers, your situation at home, and your situation at work. It might also be helpful to figure out your wants and obligations within your relationship to yourself. This could go something like this: What things do I want of myself? What things do I feel obligated to do for myself?

Keep the things you learned about these balances in mind as you read and work through the remainder of this chapter. We'll be looking at ways of thinking about interactions and relationships, and skills that will help you achieve better balance in those relationships.

GOALS IN INTERACTIONS

When Beth's husband told her that he'd had a terrible week and really wanted the two of them to go out to dinner, she immediately became anxious and irritated. She had thoughts, based on past experiences with him, that he really just wanted to go out to dinner to get her "in the mood" and that going out to dinner was just his ploy aimed at getting sex. Having thoughts that he just wanted to have sex to unwind made Beth anxious that she might not perform well enough for him. She also felt irritated that he might only want sex to relieve his stress and not because he wanted to be close to her. When they sat down for dinner, she knew she wanted to talk to him about her thoughts and feelings, but she didn't know how to begin. Her anxiety and irritation got the best of her, and she became quite critical of him. Beth confronted him about working long hours, not taking care of himself, and ignoring her. They had a long, drawn-out argument, and they ended up going home angry with each other. Later that night, still feeling angry at her husband and now angry at herself, Beth binged.

Beth wasn't used to taking the time to think through what she wanted to say to others in upsetting situations. Let's take a look at one useful way of thinking through what you might want in interpersonal situations. It's important to note that knowing what you want is no guarantee that you'll get it. But if you aren't clear about what you want, you're much less likely to get it. Approaches to helping people become more effective in relationships often emphasize being clear about goals (Gambrill and Richey 1985).

In any interpersonal situation, you have a purpose: what you want from the interaction (Linehan 1993b). You can almost always think of this as some sort of request you want the other person to fulfill or as your desire to accept or refuse another person's request of you. For example, right now we're asking you to pay attention to the ideas presented here. In a short while, we'll be requesting that you try out some of these ideas. These requests are what we want of you. Notice also that you have the choice of either accepting or refusing those requests.

But what you want to achieve in interpersonal situations isn't the only important thing. There is also your goal for how you want the other person to feel about you as a result of the interaction. This goal is about your relationship with the other person. Then there is how you want to feel about yourself—your self-goals. How you want the other person to feel about you is often about them liking you, respecting you, or appreciating you. How you want to feel about yourself is often about feeling that you've conducted yourself the best way you can or that you've been true to yourself. As authors, we hope that you respect us based on how we've approached you in this book. We also want to feel that we've been effective in how we've presented these ideas to you.

One more thing to keep in mind is that the different goals we're talking about here might be prioritized in different ways. Looking back at Beth's situation, if she had been able to use her wise mind to determine her goals, she might have had the purpose of asking her husband to listen to her concerns about sex. She might have had the goal of wanting the other person, her husband, to feel affection for her. She also had the self-goal to feel like she handled herself well in the conversation. Depending on how she understood the relative importance of her purpose, her goal for how she wanted the other person to feel about her, and the goal of how she wanted to feel about herself, she might have prioritized communicating clearly and being listened to first, her goal for how she would feel about herself second, and her goal for how her husband feels about her last. She might prioritize things in this way if she felt very upset about his behavior surrounding sex, and if she hadn't been able to handle herself well in previous conversations. This wouldn't mean that Beth didn't care how her husband felt about her. But what was more important to her in that moment was being heard and understood within the conversation. However, if her relationship had been very shaky for some time, she might have wanted to prioritize how her husband felt about her as most important, and her purpose and self-goal as second and third, respectively.

An easy way to remember these goals is to remember idea of keeping your interactions POS-itive: P for purpose, O for how you want the other person to feel about you, and S for how you want to feel about yourself. Sometimes your purpose, your goals for how you want the other person to feel about you, and how you want to feel about yourself are very clear. At other times they may not be. In cases where they aren't clear, we suggest that you use other skills. You could use wise mind or acting effectively to figure out your purpose and goals. You might also find that listing the pros and cons helps. It may not be easy to figure out your purpose and goals in some circumstances, but the more effort you put into being clear about them, the more likely you can get what you need while making your relationships stronger and better.

Practicing POS-itive Thinking

In order to get some practice, think of the last interaction you had with somebody. It could be anybody, and the interaction doesn't have to be about any sort of problem. Even if you just went through the checkout line at a department store, there's a way of thinking about your interaction with the clerk that involves POS-itive thinking. Your purpose was to get the clerk to tally up your bill. You might not have thought about it much, but you most likely conducted yourself in at least a neutral way, or you might even have been very pleasant, acting in a way that would make them like you at least a little or, at the very least, not dislike you. You probably also worked to act competently—to have your credit card or cash ready, and so on—so you could feel that you handled yourself well.

So, for that last interaction, what was your purpose (what objective did you want to accomplish or what did you want to achieve)?

_____

_____

How did you want the other person to feel about you?

_____

_____

How did you want to feel about yourself?

_____

_____

Now prioritize your purpose, your goal for how you wanted the other person to feel about you, and your goal for how you wanted to feel about yourself:

1. _____

2. _____

3. _____

Practice using these same questions to understand other interactions you've had recently. Keep in mind that many interactions might include several sets of purposes and goals as a conversation develops over time. You might start off by having the purpose of asking a friend to take care of your pet while you're away for the weekend. As the conversation evolves, your friend could then ask for advice about her boyfriend, who she's unsure about. You might then find yourself having the purpose of wanting her to listen to your concerns about her emotional welfare in a relationship that's very painful for her. So consider that you likely need to answer the above questions several times during just one interaction.

Planning to Think POS-itively

Now that you've practiced understanding conversations you've already had, try planning ahead for a discussion you intend to have in the near future. This might be a conversation with a friend, partner, coworker, supervisor, or anyone else. Choose a conversation that might be at least a bit challenging for you and think through your purpose, your goals for how the other person feels about you, and your self-goals. Use the following worksheet to help you.

What is your purpose?

_____

_____

What is your goal for how other person feels about you after the interaction?

_____

_____

What is your goal for how you want to feel about yourself after the interaction?

_____

_____

Now prioritize your purpose and goals:

1. _____

2. _____

3. _____

As you practice using the POS-itive thinking, notice if you typically prioritize one of the items over the others in most interactions, or in most interactions in particular relationships. For instance, do you typically place how the other feels about you as the top priority? Does this happen in all of your relationships or only in particular ones? Or perhaps you typically put your purpose first or your goal for how you feel about yourself last. If you do tend to repeatedly put one of the three above the others, you might want to consider changing this. Earlier in this chapter, we discussed different ways of thinking about balance in your life. Adjusting your priorities to fit just what is needed in each interaction is another way of finding balance. People who mostly put others first may have many people who like them but go without important needs and wants being met. Others who mostly put their purpose first may get a lot of what they need, but many people may dislike them and think they're selfish.

Now that you've had an opportunity to begin thinking more about your goals in interactions, it's time to move on to more skills. In this next section, we will look at skills to help you be better at achieving each of the POS-itive interpersonal goals.

SKILLS TO HELP YOU ACHIEVE YOUR PURPOSE AND GOALS

Now that you have the POS-itive thinking process to help you understand your priorities in interactions, we'll look at skills to help you achieve each of those goals by asserting yourself, responding to other people when they resist your assertion, maintaining and building relationships, and maintaining and building your self-respect.

Before we get to the actual skills, here's an illustration of them in action. In the following sections, we'll refer back to this example to understand how each of the skills can work. Jane's friend Alice made an urgent request for Jane to help her out with an event she was organizing. She wanted Jane to help her set up for the event, stay around until the end to help clean up, and then go out to a bar afterward. Jane knew that Alice had been under considerable stress lately because of problems in Alice's relationship with her boyfriend. She also knew that Alice could really use the help and support she could offer, and that Alice would probably want to get really drunk afterward. In the past, after a night of drinking Jane would commonly come home and binge on food and then purge. Jane felt uncomfortable putting herself at risk in this way, and she'd also promised her daughter that they would spend the evening together before her daughter left for college the next day. Jane knew that she couldn't back out on her daughter, but she felt that Alice had strong expectations that Jane would help her out. Past experience also told Jane that in situations like this, where she felt guilty over letting other people down, she was vulnerable to bingeing. Jane needed to use all of the interpersonal skills she had been learning to negotiate this situation effectively. Jane called Alice and talked the situation over with her. Let's take a look at their dialogue:

Jane: Alice, I just wanted to talk to you about the event on Friday night. I know that you really need my help. This is a big event for you, and things have been really stressful for you the last several weeks. At the same time, my daughter is leaving for school on Saturday, and she wanted me to spend Friday evening with her. You know how teenagers are, and she hasn't wanted to spend a lot of time with me for the last few years. Since she'll be so far away, and because she made a point of asking me, I really need to be with her on Friday. I feel bad about this, but I won't be able to help you out with your event. I would so appreciate it if you would understand.

Alice: Oh no! I don't know what I'm going to do. I was really counting on your help.

Jane: I just can't turn down my daughter, although I know that you are in a spot over this.

Alice: I mean, I'm really in a panic over this! I just know I've helped you out before...

Jane: That's true, you have been a big help before. If this were another time, I'd gladly help you out, but I just can't let my daughter down.

Alice: I know! You can bring your daughter along! You both can help me out. I'm sure she wouldn't mind at all.

Jane: Well, Alice, I don't think that's what she would really want to do. It's important to me that I do what she wants. She'll be away for a long time without us seeing each other. Look, Alice, your friendship is important to me. I know you need help, and I know this event is important to you. What I can do is come over to the studio early and help you set up. I can't be there for the event, but if you want to wait until the next morning to clean up, I can come back then. Would that work?

Alice: That would be great if you could do that. I know you would help out more if you could.

Now that we have the example of Jane and Alice's interaction, let's look at some of the skills involved.

Interpersonal Purpose Skills

Interpersonal purpose skills will help you achive your objective in an interaction. This is about getting what you want. Later we'll cover skills for your goals of how you want the other person to feel about you and how you want to feel about yourself. So keep in mind that our focus for now is on helping you get what you want. There are two categories of interpersonal purpose skills: assertion skills to help you ask for what you want or refuse unwanted requests, and response skills to help you handle resistance to your assertiveness. In the preceding dialogue, Jane made a refusal to Alice's request that she help out with the event, and she also had to respond to Alice's resistance to her refusal.

ASSERTION SKILLS

There are three main skills for asserting yourself. The first is explaining yourself, the second is asserting yourself, and the third is rewarding the other person in advance for giving you what you want (Bower and Bower 1980; Linehan 1993b). Explaining yourself involves letting the other person know what the situation is that prompts your request or refusal and your feelings or opinions about the situation. The idea here is that the other person will be more likely to give you what you want if they understand your situation. Jane explained to Alice the situation with her daughter's request and how important it was for Jane to grant this request. She noted that it was important not just because her daughter was going away to school, but also because she hadn't spent a lot of time with her daughter in the last few years.

Asserting yourself involves telling the other person clearly what it is you're asking for or refusing. The person won't necessarily know what you want, even if they understand the situation you're in. Although Alice may have been able to understand that Jane was refusing her request just through Jane's explanation of her situation, Jane made it clear to Alice by stating specifically that she couldn't help out. Asserting yourself is especially important when you're making a request of another person. Don't assume that other people will know what you want!

Rewarding the other person involves figuring out and explaining how that person might benefit from giving you what you want. The idea here is that the other person will be more likely to agree to your request or understand your refusal if they see that they'll benefit in some way too. A very simple way of doing this is to say that you would really appreciate it if the other person complied with your request. This is what Jane did with Alice. There are many other ways that you can do this. For example, in asking a supervisor for additional time to complete a project, you might say that having more time would help you to make sure you did the best possible job. If the project is important to the supervisor, doing the best possible job would be a reward.

RESPONSE SKILLS

Response skills help you handle situations where other people might resist giving you what you want or accepting your refusal. These skills include confidence, persistence, fogging, and negotiation.

Confidence involves responding in a way that communicates both strength and nondefensiveness (Gambrill and Richey 1985; Linehan 1993b). The idea here is that those who are reluctant to give you what you want may be more hesitant to refuse or attack if you communicate strength and nondefensiveness. Jane was direct with Alice, communicating confidence. She also responded nondefensively when

Alice argued that she had helped Jane in the past. This was a point where Jane could have gone on the defensive. Instead, she used skills that we will discuss below.

Persistence is the skill of firmly repeating what you want over and over again (Linehan 1993b). This skill has been part of assertiveness training from very early in its development. A term for this technique, "broken record," refers back to the days of vinyl records that would skip and repeat the same thing over and over (Smith 1975). The idea here is that people who resist your assertiveness may offer reasons why they can't comply or why you shouldn't assert yourself, or they may act in such a way that they divert you from your request. Persistence involves returning, like that old-time vinyl record that skips, over and over again to your request. Persistence means that you don't get caught up in refuting the other person's arguments, defending yourself, or responding to diversions—you simply repeat your request over and over. When you get caught up in attempting to refute the other person's arguments, you take on the burden of coming up with reasons why that argument is false. If you keep on attempting this, they can eventually wear you down. However, if you simply repeat your request or refusal over and over, you can wear them down. Rather then counterattacking Alice when she told Jane she had helped her out in the past, Jane used fogging (see below) and repeatedly returned to her refusal. Remembering that she could use persistence helped her stay nondefensive and let her avoid counterattacking.

Fogging involves briefly acknowledging some element of truth in the other person's resistance without giving up your request (Smith 1975). This skill goes hand in hand with persistence. In our example, Jane acknowledged that Alice was "in a spot over this." Even more importantly, when Alice brought up the fact that she had helped Jane in the past, Jane used fogging by acknowledging that this was true. The key here is that you can agree with someone's point without necessarily giving up your own.

Even though you may effectively assert yourself and respond to resistance with persistence and fogging, you may find yourself in the position of needing to negotiate (Linehan 1993b; Smith 1975). This can be important to keep in mind when you're asserting yourself with people who are very persistent themselves, who have power or authority over you, or who are important to you in other ways. Alice's friendship is important to Jane. In the end, Jane was willing to negotiate with Alice so that Jane could spend time with her daughter and still be available to help to Alice. Skillful negotiation often involves the willingness to give up a little to get what you want and to communicate this idea to the other person when you can. Jane offered to come over early and help set up the event, and she suggested to Alice that she might wait until Saturday to clean up so Jane could pitch in. Negotiation isn't always possible, and the other person may not always be willing. Nevertheless, this can be an important skill for helping you achieve your interpersonal purpose.

PURPOSE SKILLS PRACTICE WORKSHEET

The following worksheet will help you practice your purpose skills. We suggest that you photocopy the worksheet so that you can use it both for interactions you've already had that you wish you'd handled differently and for planning how to address problems you haven't discussed yet and will want to in the future.

Write out how you wanted to or will want to explain the situation to the other person. Describe the facts first of all.

_____

_____

_____

Write out your opinions and feelings about the situation. Use "I think…" and "I feel…" statements.

_____

_____

_____

Write out your request or your refusal. Make what you are saying clear.

_____

_____

_____

What reward is there for the other person to grant your request or allow your refusal? How can you communicate this?

_____

_____

_____

Now let's work on your response skills. How would you communicate confidence? What would your tone of voice be? What would your body language be like?

_____

_____

_____

_____

Write down some of the things you think the other person might say to resist your request or refusal.

_____

_____

_____

_____

_____

_____

How would you use fogging to respond to each statement of resistance above? How would you return to your original request or refusal using persistence?

_____

_____

_____

_____

_____

_____

If you need to negotiate, what would you give up in order to get what you want? What would the other person need to do in order for the negotiation to work?

_____

_____

_____

_____

_____

_____

More Skills to Help Build and Maintain Your Relationships

Next we'll discuss further skills for maintaining and building relationships. The interpersonal purpose skills we just covered can assist you in maintaining and building relationships by helping you to get more of what you want and need. When you don't get enough of what you want and need, your relationships will suffer. On the other hand, asserting yourself in order to get what you want and need can be stressful for the other person. The relationship skills we'll look at now are active listening and expressing feelings of concern and caring about the other person (Gambrill and Richey 1985). Balancing your efforts to get what you want and need by expressing concern and caring will help to maintain and build your relationships.

Active listening involves attending and communicating interest. As you may already know or intuit, there are specific behaviors that you can use to communicate to the other person that their opinions, ideas, and involvement with you are important. If you don't actively communicate these things to that person, the likelihood that they will understand their importance to you is low.

Active listening involves body language and validating what the other person is saying. Associated body language includes facing the other person, making eye contact, and doing things like nodding your head as you understand what they say to you. In our example, you'll recall that Jane was talking to Alice on the phone, so her body language wasn't critical. Jane did use validation when she noted that not helping Alice would leave Alice "in a spot." By openly saying this, Jane communicated to Alice that she was listening. Even when Jane used the skill of fogging, she paraphrased Alice by acknowledging that Alice had helped Jane in the past. When a person hears what they have said paraphrased back to them, it can help them see that they've been understood. The result is usually that the person feels validated. Validation also includes acknowledging the truth in what another is saying. Once again, when Jane used the skill of fogging, she was also validating the fact that Alice had helped her out in the past. Validation doesn't mean that you have the same opinion as another person. It's possible to acknowledge what another has said without abandoning your view. If Alice had accused Jane of ignoring her need, Jane could have responded, "I can see how you would feel that way since I can't help you out with this." By saying this, Jane wouldn't be saying that she really *is* ignoring Alice. Rather, Jane's validation would acknowledge Alice's statement and help her feel understood. Jane could still express Alice's importance to her while asserting herself.

Expressing feelings of concern and caring about the other person is just that—directly letting them know their importance to you. While you can use active listening skills with anyone, expressing feelings of concern and caring is most useful with people you are close to emotionally or would like to get closer to. Jane told Alice directly that their friendship was important to her. Saying this increased the likelihood that they could maintain their relationship even though Jane was making a difficult refusal. By listening actively and expressing concern and caring, you will be better able to balance your purpose with your desire to build or maintain the relationship.

Practicing Listening and Expressing Care

Answer the following questions to get practice using these relationship skills. You can use the situation in the purpose skills practice you did above or answer the same questions for a new situation.

What body language will you use as part of active listening?

_____

_____

_____

As you think of the other person's possible responses to your request or refusal, how would you validate their statements?

_____

_____

_____

_____

_____

If this relationship is important to you, what feelings of concern or caring could you express in this situation?

_____

_____

_____

_____

_____

_____

Building and Maintaining Your Relationship with Yourself

You can also use each of the skills in this chapter to help you maintain and improve the relationship you have with yourself. By achieving your purpose in interactions more often, you can feel more confidence. Taking care of relationships more effectively will also help you gain greater confidence.

However, there are several more skills that are important in helping you develop your self-esteem, self-respect, and self-efficacy. These skills are truthfulness, valued action, and self-validation (Gambrill and Richey 1985: Linehan 1993b).

Truthfulness involves acting honestly with yourself and with others about the big things in life. Being dishonest about important things can leave you feeling guilty and embarrassed. While honesty can be difficult in the short run, living truthfully can help you feel greater strength over time. Looking back at Jane and Alice, Jane could have made up an excuse for not helping Alice out. She might have waited until the day of the event and called Alice saying she was very ill. This strategy might have worked to get Alice to back off, but it likely would have left Jane feeling guilty. Instead, Jane honestly and directly explained her situation and what she wanted. Although this was harder in the short run, it was important practice for Jane in becoming more assertive and effective in her relationships and in feeling better about herself.

Valued action is behavior that moves you in the direction of your values. Some common values include being loyal and trustworthy, financial success, hard work, having others like you, having others respect you, health, meaningful relationships, playtime, power, relaxation time, spirituality, and wisdom. These are not the same as goals, which you expect to achieve one day and be done. Values are things that are important to you that you work on over your lifetime. Having good family relations, for example, takes continuing work. Jane valued her relationship with her daughter. If she had abandoned her daughter's request, she would have felt bad because she wouldn't have been living up to her value of being close to her daughter. Jane also valued her friendship with Alice. She pursued valued action with her daughter by refusing Alice's initial request and fulfilling her daughter's request. She pursued valued action with Alice by expressing her caring for Alice and negotiating a way to help her out.

Self-validation is acknowledging the value in yourself, your thoughts, your feelings, and your behavior. Just as validating another person helps them feel understood, validating yourself can help you feel valued. One of the first steps in building self-validation is noticing when you act in ways that invalidate yourself. Next, consider how you would acknowledge the importance of yourself and your thoughts, feelings, and behavior. Consider that the act of using interpersonal purpose skills is one of self-validation. For instance, Jane could have invalidated herself by simply granting Alice's request without thinking about herself, her purpose, her valued action, and her daughter. Giving in when others resist your attempts to assert yourself can also be self-invalidating. If Jane had agreed when Alice asserted that she'd been helpful to Jane in the past and added to this acquiescence by saying, "I know I'm just a terrible friend... I don't know why you put up with me," she would have been invalidating herself. In particular, she would have been invalidating herself if she actually believed that she hadn't been a terrible friend. Jane might have said something like this in the heat of the moment, while feeling uncomfortable with Alice's reaction and with her own refusal of Alice's request. But for Jane to say she had been a terrible friend if she truly didn't believe it would be self-invalidating. On the other hand, if Jane believed she *had* been a terrible friend, it would be self-invalidating to say say otherwise. In self-validation, as in all the other skills, it helps to use your wise mind. Don't attempt to validate what you know is untruthful for you. This is important to keep in mind as you are working toward separating from Ed mind. When in Ed mind, you might attempt to validate what Ed tells you is true, even though we've established that Ed mind isn't based in truth or logic.

Self-Relationship Skills Practice

Now it's time to answer the following questions to get practice using self-relationship skills. Use the situation in the purpose skills practice you did above, or answer the same questions for a new situation.

What will you need to say or do to act truthfully in this situation?

_____

_____

_____

What values of yours are important in this situation? What will you need to do to pursue valued action?

_____

_____

_____

_____

How might you think or act in a way that is self-invalidating in this situation? What will you need to do to act in a way that's self-validating?

_____

_____

_____

_____

_____

WHAT INTERFERES WITH INTERPERSONAL EFFECTIVENESS?

Before we finish this chapter, we should take some time to explain what might get in the way of acting skillfully and effectively in relationships. Being aware of what might interfere with your use of these skills will help you develop strategies for dealing with these blocks, making it easier for you to get the results you want (Gambrill and Richey 1985; Linehan 1993b).

First of all, not knowing what to say or do in a relationship can be a huge problem. In this chapter, we've offered a number of ways of thinking about relationships and a number of skills that can help you figure out what to say or do. Also, remember to use wise mind and pros and cons to help you figure out what to do. We realize that there could still be many situations where these skills may not give you the ideas you need. We encourage you to check out the many useful books available on the market today about relationships. We also encourage you to seek advice from trusted friends and coworkers, and from counselors, clergy, and therapists. Use whatever resources you have available to you.

Worries about what other people will say or do can also get in your way. You may worry that you won't be liked, that the other person will get mad as you assert yourself, or any number of other worries. These kinds of concerns happen even more frequently in Ed mind. Again, use your wise mind to assess these worries. Observe or describe your worries mindfully and then let them go. Be clear in your wise mind how likely it is that your worries will come to pass. In other words, be mindful of the influence of Ed mind. Consider in your wise mind how you would be able to cope with the worries if they did come to pass. Actively cope. Use encouraging and cheerleading statements to help yourself act effectively in relationships. Respond skillfully to your worry thoughts rather than allowing them to take charge of your actions.

Emotions might also get in the way of acting skillfully in relationships. You might find yourself feeling guilty for asking for what you want. You might feel fear that something terrible could happen and stop yourself from being assertive. Use all of the emotion regulation skills to help yourself out. Use your wise mind to assess whether your emotions are justified or unjustified. If they're unjustified, use opposite action by noticing your urge to not assert yourself, and then assert yourself anyway. If your emotions get so intense that you can't control your urges to binge, purge, or use other problem behaviors, use distress tolerance. Respond skillfully to your emotions rather than allowing them to take charge of your actions.

Finally, recognize that sometimes other people will be completely unwilling to give you what you want or need or may make getting what you want very painful. Try to see that this might happen even if you have been as skillful as you (or as anyone) can be. Understand that while you might not achieve your interpersonal purpose, this doesn't mean that you can't achieve your other relationship or self-relationship goals. The other person may even get very angry with you—this still doesn't mean that you didn't act skillfully. If you're faced with anger, we suggest that you turn to your self-relationship skills to help you feel better about the interaction. When others are uncooperative, think about using radical acceptance. It may be painful, but you *can* reduce your suffering.

Responding to Things That Interfere

Answer the following questions to get practice responding to things that may interfere with using relationship skills and achieving your purpose. Use the situation in the purpose skills practice you did above, or answer the questions below for a new situation.

Are you unsure about what you need to say or do to act skillfully in this situation? Have you thought through the interpersonal purpose, relationship, and self-relationship skills? Where else can you go to get ideas?

_____

_____

_____

_____

What worry thoughts might get in the way in this situation? What will you need to do to respond skillfully to them?

_____

_____

_____

_____

What emotions might get in the way in this situation? What will you need to do to respond skillfully to them?

_____

_____

_____

_____

Even if you don't achieve your purpose in this situation, how will you have used relationship skills effectively?

_____

_____

_____

_____

If you don't achieve your purpose in this situation and the other person is upset with you, how will you have used self-relationship skills effectively?

_____

_____

_____

_____

If you don't achieve your purpose in this situation, how can you use radical acceptance?

_____

_____

_____

_____

CONCLUSION

In this chapter, we looked at ways of thinking about and achieving greater balance in relationships. We discussed a way of thinking about goals in interactions—the POS-itive thinking process. Then we looked at skills for becoming better at achieving each of those goals. Finally, we looked at what might interfere with using relationship skills. In the next chapter, we'll take a look at how to put together the skills you've been learning and the behavior analyses you did earlier in the book. This will give you a clearer idea of how you can use each of the skills you've learned to break the cycle of bingeing and purging and move toward a life that is fuller and more satisfying—a life worth being present in.

CHAPTER 9

Weaving Solutions

In the last four chapters you learned about mindfulness, emotion regulation, distress tolerance, and interpersonal skills. You've had opportunities to practice using the skills and have probably already begun to work on changing some of your bulimic and other problem behaviors. In this chapter, we're going to take a look at a systematic way of applying the skills you've learned to the information you gathered in chapter 2 (What Is DBT?) and chapter 4 (Understanding Your Patterns). In this chapter, we'll look at how your problem behaviors function in the patterns you identified in chapters 2 and 4 and which skills can be most helpful in breaking those patterns. You might want to take a look back at chapter 4 to review the elements of behavior analysis.

First, let's understand what we mean by "function." How a particular behavior functions in a pattern of behaviors is basically about three things:

1.   What vulnerabilities may make you more prone to the behavior (see chapter 6)

2.   What thoughts, feelings, behaviors, or events come immediately before and trigger the behavior in question (determine this using behavior analysis)

3.   What are the short- and long-term consequences of the behavior in question (also determined using behavior analysis)

As an example, let's look at Ted's experience with behavior analysis. After an incident of bingeing, he came to understand how his problem eating functioned for him. Before the incident, Ted had a poor night's sleep and a very stressful day at work. He met his girlfriend, Anne, at his house for dinner. Anne told him she was going out with an old friend from college, Beth, and would be spending the night at her apartment, and Ted noticed that this was when he first became scared. He then had thoughts about what a bad influence this friend had been on Anne in the past and started to feel angry. He commented to Anne that her friend was always trouble and immediately felt some relief. Anne then became upset with him and left. Ted felt increased fear and had the thought "She was just waiting for me to say something so she could leave and go out with Beth." After having this thought, Ted felt angry and wanted to go after Anne and confront her. Instead, he went into the kitchen and started eating. He noticed that while he was eating, he no longer felt scared or angry. Afterward, however, he felt physically sick and angry at himself for having eaten so much. He also realized that Anne had always been trustworthy in their relationship and had never given him a reason to doubt her.

As Ted looked over this analysis, he saw that his bingeing functioned as a response to anger and possibly to fear, as well as being a behavior that gave him relief from those feelings—at least in the short run. He also noted that, in the long run, bingeing left him feeling physically sick and angry with himself. Ted also noted that a poor night's sleep and stressful workday probably made him more prone to this behavior. He didn't always binge on days he felt tired and stressed from work, but he understood that these factors made him more vulnerable to reacting to Anne so strongly.

SOLUTIONS AND BEHAVIOR ANALYSIS

Now that we've looked at Ted's behavior analysis, it's time to look at the steps for weaving solutions into a behavior analysis. We've listed the steps in brief below, and we'll follow with a section exploring each of these steps in more detail. Keep in mind that, as we go, we'll help you identify skills to assist you with major problem behaviors, as well as other problem or ineffective behaviors that are related to the major problem behaviors you've settled on as targets for yourself. Because you're reading this book, major problem behaviors likely include bulimic behaviors like bingeing, purging, and restricting. Other related problematic or ineffective behaviors could be most anything else that doesn't work for you. These might include having judgmental thoughts, being unable to assert yourself, or acting in an aggressive way that strains relationships. Ted's major problem behavior was bingeing. But as he looked at his behavior analysis, he understood that he made judgmental statements about Beth that ended up being part of the chain of behaviors leading to his binge.

Keep the distinction between major problem behaviors and related problematic and ineffective behaviors in mind as we go through the steps in the following sections. While you might not do a detailed analysis for all of the problem behaviors you identify in a chain, be sure to at least use the following steps to come up with solutions that address the prompting event and the major problem behavior. Be aware that the more thorough you are in coming up with solutions for your other problematic and ineffective behaviors, the more likely it is that you can break the patterns of behavior that have troubled you for so long.

Steps for Generating Solutions

Here are the steps for identifying problem or ineffective behaviors and for generating solutions to help with those behaviors (solution analysis). We will look at each of these steps in more detail in subsequent sections.

1. Identify ineffective and problem behaviors.

2. For as many ineffective or problem behaviors as you can, identify what event in the environment or what thought, feeling, or behavior came just before the ineffective or problem behavior.

3.   Think of each ineffective or problem behavior as actually an attempt to solve a problem presented by whatever happened just before that behavior.

4.   Identify skills that can help you respond to that problem more effectively. These skills can help you prevent or decrease how often you engage in the ineffective or problem behaviors.

5.   Identify what happened immediately after the ineffective or problem behavior.

6.   Figure out if what happened immediately after the behavior was something that had a desirable or positive outcome for you. If this is the case, figure out what skill would help you get the same desirable or positive outcome.

7.   Identify the susceptibilities that made you more prone to engaging in the major problem behavior you're analyzing. Decide which emotion regulation skills would help you with those susceptibilities.

8.   Make a plan to use the skills you decide on the next time you find yourself in a similar situation.

9.   Troubleshoot your plan. What might get in the way of using skills instead of problem behaviors? What skills would help you respond to each of these obstacles?

10.   Add your troubleshooting skills to your plan.

11.   Make a commitment to yourself to carry out this plan.

Identifying Ineffective or Problem Behaviors

So far we've focused on bingeing, purging, restricting, and other problem behaviors related to eating. These behaviors are why you picked up this book. The skills and strategies we've covered so far can be used to help you reduce or eliminate these behaviors. However, if you look closely at some of the behavior analyses you've done so far, you may be able to find other ineffective or problem behaviors that are part of the chain of events leading to bulimic behaviors. You can use skills you've learned in this book to help you with any other ineffective or problem behavior in your analyses. Breaking any link in the chain can help you disrupt the whole thing. In practice, it may take using multiple skills for multiple problem behaviors along the chain to help you not engage in bulimic behaviors. We want to help you find as many opportunities to break these patterns as possible.

Let's look again at Ted's example. One way of looking at his behavior analysis can suggest that his bingeing wasn't the only problematic behavior he engaged in. His fear in response to Anne's news that she would be spending time with Beth may not have been justified. His thoughts about Beth being a bad influence may have been unfounded. Beth may not have been a bad influence, and Anne might be very capable of making good decisions for herself. Ted's comment to Anne about Beth being trouble seemed to have been an unskillful way of handling his feelings and the situation. The same goes for some of his subsequent emotions, thoughts, and actions. More skillful behavior along the way may have helped Ted prevent the binge.

Sometimes it can be fairly obvious when a behavior is ineffective or problematic, but often it's complicated. There's no simple rule to follow, but we will offer you some guidelines. As you become aware of any given moment in life, and as you become skilled in behavior analysis, it's helpful to ask yourself what your wise-mind goal is or was at the time. Effective behaviors move you toward your wise-mind goals, and toward a life that's worth being present in. Ineffective and problem behaviors tend to move you away from your wise-mind goals, and away from a life that's worth being present in.

How do you figure out what moves you toward these important goals? It's not necessarily what your emotion mind is telling you to do. If you're feeling strong emotions, ask yourself if it's a manifestation of emotion mind. If you're responding to or feeling strong emotions, it also can be helpful to use wise mind to understand whether the feeling is justified or unjustified.

Effective action is definitely not what Ed mind is telling you to do. Notice whether or not you are in Ed mind and take some steps to get into wise mind. It can help, as we discussed in chapter 3, to remember your purpose.

If you're dealing with an interpersonal situation, figure out what your POS-itive goals are using wise mind. In general, part of this comes down to understanding how to handle the immediate situation you are in while keeping important long-term goals in mind.

Identifying Ineffective and Problem Behaviors

It's useful at this point to get some practice in identifying ineffective and problem behaviors. You may want to use a behavior analysis you did in chapter 4, or use the exercises in that chapter to do a new behavior analysis. For each behavior you engaged in, including thoughts, feelings, and outward behavior, ask yourself the following questions. (This is a mental problem-solving process, so we have not included space here to respond.)

1. At this point in the chain of events, what would your wise-mind goal be?

2. Did the behavior you engaged in move you toward that wise-mind goal or toward a life that's worth being present in?

3. If the answer to the preceding questions is no, is it accurate for you to say that this behavior was ineffective or a problem?

4. If so, note this as a problem or ineffective behavior.

5. Now, move on to the next behavior in the chain and repeat this sequence of questions. Continue until you've analyzed each behavior, including the last major bulimic behavior in the chain.

This is difficult work to do and can be very tedious. If you get discouraged, keep in mind that the purpose here is to give you as many opportunities as possible to break the patterns of behavior you've been stuck in for a long time. If you find yourself stalled and unable to determine if a particular behavior is ineffective or a problem, move on to the next behavior. Now let's move on to the next step of solution analysis.

Identifying the Problems You Were Trying to Solve

Figuring out what problem is being solved by an ineffective or problematic behavior can help you determine which skills might be most useful at any point in a chain of behaviors. Let's look again at Ted's example. His unjustified fear at Anne's news that she would be spending time with Beth functioned to motivate him to take action in response to a perceived threat—that Anne might do something to damage Ted's relationship with her because of Beth's influence. His thoughts about Beth being a bad influence may have functioned in a similar way. His comment to Anne that Beth was always trouble functioned as an attempt to eliminate the threat and reduce his fear and anger by influencing Anne to stay away from Beth. By acting on these thoughts and emotions, Ted felt some immediate relief. Of course, this relief was only momentary, because Anne stormed off and Ted found himself feeling fear again.

Problematic or ineffective behaviors often function to reduce a painful emotion, solve some problem in the environment, or both. Reviewing chapter 6 will help you determine what problems your emotional responses may be solutions for. Keep in mind, as we noted in the preceding section, that unjustified emotions may be solutions to a problem that isn't really there. In Ted's example, Anne had never given him reason to distrust her. His fear and anger were unjustified and were attempts to solve a problem or threat that really wasn't there. Consider that one emotion can sometimes be solving the problem of feeling another painful emotion. In Ted's example, he quickly went from feeling fear to feeling anger. One way of understanding the function of Ted's anger is that it served to reduce his fear. Once again, use your wise mind to understand what's truly going on so that you can see what problem your behaviors are attempting to solve.

What Problems Are Your Behaviors Trying to Solve?

Return to the behavior analysis you were using in the last section. For each ineffective or problem behavior you identified, answer the following questions:

1. If your behavior was functioning to solve a problem in the environment, what was that problem?

2. If your behavior was functioning to solve the problem of a painful emotion, what was the emotion?

3. Is your behavior solving both of these types of problem?

Skills to Substitute for Problem Behaviors

Now that you've identified ineffective and problem behaviors and the problems you were using them to solve, let's move on to the task of determining which skills might work well for reducing those behaviors. Which skills might be useful substitutes for problem or ineffective behaviors depends mostly on two factors: the type of problem behavior, and what it's trying to solve. Problem or ineffective behaviors usually consist of three types: thoughts, emotions (including urges), and behaviors.

Here's a list of skills that can be helpful in changing ineffective or problem thoughts:

Mindfulness skills:

- Noticing

- Labeling

- Equanimity

- One thing at a time

- Wise mind

Distress tolerance skills:

- Statements of self-support

Here's a list of skills that can be helpful in changing ineffective or problem emotions:

Emotion regulation skills:

- Mindfulness of emotions

- Doing the opposite of emotionally motivated urges

Distress tolerance skills:

- BOSS

- Learning to soothe yourself with sight, sounds, smell, and touch

- Tolerating distress by finding another focus (happy place, higher power, purpose, relaxation, self-encouraging statements)

- Tolerating distress by focusing on values

- Tolerating distress by focusing on being present in the moment

- Radical acceptance

Here's a list of skills that can be helpful in changing ineffective or problematic behaviors:

Mindfulness skills:

- Acting effectively

- Wise mind

Interpersonal effectiveness skills:

- Finding balance

- POS-itive thinking

- Interpersonal purpose

Emotion regulation skills:

- Acting opposite to emotionally motivated urges

Distress tolerance skills:

- BOSS

General problem-solving skills:

- Generating alternative solutions

- Looking at the pros and cons of each solution

- Choosing a solution to implement

- Deciding what you need to implement the solution

- Making a plan to implement the solution

- Doing it

- Evaluating the outcome

Identifying Skills for More Effective Problem Solving

Now that we've gone over suggested skills for solving problems that precede ineffective or problematic behaviors, the next step is to list skills that you can use for each of the problems those ineffective and problematic behaviors are attempting to solve. Use the same behavior analysis you've been working with in this chapter. Referring to the list provided above, list which skills could be useful.

_____

_____

_____

_____

_____

_____

_____

_____

_____

_____

Next, give yourself a plan for using each skill. If you decided upon skills that need to be used in the moment a situation is happening (for instance, using interpersonal skills in an argument), give yourself an opportunity to practice using those skills. *Imaginal practice* is one effective way of doing that. This means that you practice using the skills in your imagination. Here are the steps involved in imaginal practice:

1. Imagine yourself in the situation in which you needed to or will need to use the skills.

2. Imagine it as vividly and realistically as possible, including your emotional reactions and the reactions of people around you.

3. Imagine yourself using the skill. If it would be difficult to use the skill in real life, include this difficulty in the way you imagine the situation.

4. Repeat this several times.

If you decided that there's a skill you can use now, one that doesn't need to be used in the situation itself, use it as soon as you are able. General problem solving is an example of a skill that you could work on now. Let's look at an example of using a skill outside of the situation. Say you have an argument with your partner about finances and it's a prompting event for bingeing and purging. In between the argument and the bingeing and purging, you think about your finances and realize that there's a serious problem going on with your money. In this case, you'd want to use general problem-solving skills as soon as you can to address the problem. The more you effectively address problems in your life as soon as you can, the more likely it is that you'll feel better and do better.

Before moving on to the next section, be sure that you've followed the steps in this section to come up with solutions for your major problem behavior in your behavior analysis, as well as for the prompting event. This is the minimum that you can do to break your patterns of bulimic behavior. Keep in mind that the more behaviors you have solutions for, the better.

Problem or Ineffective Behaviors That Lead to Desirable Outcomes

Now we'll figure out which problem behaviors are followed immediately by consequences that might reinforce that ineffective or problem behavior. This is important because positive or desirable consequences that immediately follow a problem behavior make the behavior more likely to occur in the future. In behavioral psychology, this principle is referred to as *reinforcement*. Reinforcement happens all the time for everyday behaviors. You push the button for the elevator, and the elevator arrives. Your button-pressing behavior is reinforced by the arrival of the elevator. The next time you need an elevator, you're more likely to press a button. Think about it: if elevators stopped coming, you would soon stop pressing the button.

It's important to note that reinforcement works whether we're aware of it or not and whether we intend for the outcome to happen or not. As an example, Michael was under a deadline to hand in a report at work. His printer wasn't working properly. Every time he tried to print out the report, the paper jammed. He attempted to print over and over, but he couldn't get the printer to work. Out of desperation, he tried all kinds of things, including opening the blinds on the window next to the printer. On the next try, the report printed out! You know what he found himself doing the rest of the week? Each time he needed to print, he opened the blinds. He wasn't even aware of doing this at first, and he certainly didn't consciously reason that opening the blinds would make the printer work—but he still found himself opening those blinds. So it's important to remember that positive or desirable consequences can and do influence your behavior, whether you intend it or are even aware of it.

Let's return to Ted's example to see more instances of how problem behaviors can be reinforced. When Ted felt angry about Anne's plans to spend time with Beth, he made a critical statement about Beth to Anne. He immediately felt relief. In doing solution analysis, Ted needs to consider that his critical remarks might be reinforced by that feeling of relief. This payoff could mean that Ted will continue to use this behavior in the future, and it may become more frequent. When Ted started eating, he no longer felt scared or angry. Ted also needs to consider that his binge behavior might be reinforced by feelings of relief.

What makes consequences reinforcing isn't always clear. Getting relief from a painful emotion can be reinforcing. So if you feel stressed and bingeing numbs you out, then the numbing can be reinforcing. But being numb isn't reinforcing for everyone. Yelling at someone you feel angry with can get them to leave your immediate presence. The other person leaving can be reinforcing—or not. For some people in some situations, getting the person who prompted anger to leave is desirable. For others or in other situations, getting the person to leave can feel threatening or lead to guilt. For some people, having others express concern about a binge can be desirable; for others it can be embarrassing. For some people who feel hurt by criticism, having the thought "How dare they say that?" followed by feelings of anger can be reinforcing. This might happen because the hurt goes away, even though anger takes its place.

In general, as you identify which ineffective or problem behaviors have reinforcing outcomes, it will be important to consider behaviors that are followed by changes in emotional state, changes in thought content or social responses. Here are some of the potential reinforcing outcomes in each category:

Changes in emotional state

- That generate pleasurable emotions

- That bring relief from painful emotions

- That at least reduce painful emotions somewhat

- That change the emotional state from one painful emotion to another painful emotion, particularly if the second painful emotion is easier to tolerate than the first (for instance, feeling angry rather than hurt)

Changes in thought content

- That eliminate distressing thoughts and topics of thinking

- That exchange one distressing thought or topic for another, particularly if the second thought or topic is more tolerable than the first

Social responses

- That involve displays of caring or concern

- That lead to any attention at all, particularly when you aren't be getting much contact or attention from a particular person, or from people in general, much of the time

While these are not the only possible reinforcing consequences of behaviors, this list covers the most likely reinforcers you will encounter.

Finally, we should be clear that you can only truly tell if a behavior is reinforced by its consequences by observing the behavior over and over again and observing how it changes if the consequences change. Figuring this out can be very difficult even for highly training therapists, so you may find it pretty tough. The full analysis may not even be necessary. If you have a suspicion that a behavior is reinforced by its consequences, that may be enough to let you know that working on skills may be helpful.

Identifying Ineffective or Problem Behaviors That Lead to Reinforcing Outcomes

Return to the behavior analysis you've been using and the ineffective or problem behaviors you have identified previously. For each of these behaviors, ask yourself if it is followed by a desired or positive change in emotional state or thoughts or a positive or desired social response. List each behavior that might be under these types of reinforcement.

_____

_____

_____

_____

_____

_____

_____

_____

Identifying Skills with Outcomes Similar to Problem Behaviors

The principle for selecting skills that will help bring about the same or similar outcomes is based on understanding how different skills can be expected to work. Here are some general guidelines about categories of skills and outcomes:

Emotion regulation skills:

- Help generate pleasurable emotions

- Help you understand and become aware of emotions

- Bring relief from or reduce painful emotions

Mindfulness skills:

- Make thoughts less distressing and keep topics of thought from dragging on

- Help change thoughts (for example, changing judgments to a stance of equanimity)

Interpersonal skills:

- Increase desirable or positive social outcomes

Distress tolerance skills:

- Distract attention from problems you cannot solve, or cannot solve right now

To return to Ted's example, if Ted understands that his critical statements might lead to relief from fear, he could consider using the emotion regulation skill of mindfulness of the current emotion instead. Using this skill, he would work to observe his emotion, label it as fear, feel it like a wave, remember that he is more than his emotion, and not act on his fear. Taking these steps can help him experience relief without making a critical remark.

Let's take a look at an important point here: Even when problematic behaviors might have immediate reinforcing consequences, they almost always have long-term undesirable or painful consequences. Even though Ted felt immediate relief by making a critical remark about Beth, he had to deal with Anne becoming upset as a result. As we've discussed (and as is likely clear from your own behavior analysis), bulimic behaviors also have negative long-term consequences of feeling out of control, feeling guilt and shame, and so on. So another important skill for helping with problem behaviors that might be reinforced by short-term consequences is to remind yourself of the longer-term negative consequences. The key here is to learn how to make yourself aware of the long-term consequences as you find yourself beginning to engage in a behavior. Doing this can help prevent you from engaging in the behavior and reduce the reinforcing quality of the positive or desirable short-term consequences. However, reminding yourself of long-term negative consequences after you've engaged in the behavior won't help you directly change the behavior, and ruminating on it later can make things worse. While reminding yourself of negative consequences alone is often not enough, this can be an additional skill to help you reduce and eliminate problem behaviors.

Identifying Skills to Generate Similar Outcomes to Ineffective or Problem Behaviors

Return to the list you made in the previous exercise, of ineffective or problem behaviors that are followed by desirable or positive outcomes. For each of these behaviors, select a skill or skills from the above list of skills and outcomes that can help you generate the same or similar outcomes. Use the imaginal practice we discussed above to help you practice using each of these skills. Make a commitment to yourself to use them the next time you are in the same or similar circumstances. Write down each specific skill and the outcome it can help with.

_____

_____

_____

_____

_____

_____

_____

_____

_____

Skills for Susceptibility

If you understand the emotion regulation skill of attending to physiological balance, then this part is simple. For each of the susceptibility factors you noted in your behavior analysis, identify which physiological balance skill or skills would be helpful. Make a plan to work on these balances on a regular basis—preferably every day. If you don't remember much about these skills, go back to chapter 6, on emotion regulation, and reread that section.

Make a Plan, Troubleshoot, and Commit

It can be helpful at this point to summarize what problem behaviors you've identified and what skills you figured out might be helpful to you. You've probably done a lot of work so far, but making a summary list at this point would help. List the problem behaviors, and underneath each, the skills you'll use to change them. Do this on a separate piece of paper now.

You're almost finished with your solution analysis. Take the summary that you just wrote and think about what might get in the way of you using the skills you listed. Here are some factors that might interfere:

- In the heat of the moment, forgetting what you decided to do

- Feeling unwilling to use skills when you need to

- Other people making it difficult for you to be skillful (for example, intentionally or unintentionally encouraging you to engage in problem behaviors or intentionally or unintentionally punishing you for using skills)

At the end of your summary, list what might interfere, along with additional solutions for those interfering factors. Here are some suggested solutions for each of the above types of interfering factors:

Forgetting

- Go over your plan every day for a week or more.

- Carry a copy of your plan with you wherever you go so you can pull it out if you need it.

- Use cues to help you to remember: tie a string around your finger, put on an unfamiliar piece of jewelry, carry an object around in your pocket to remind yourself, put a sign up with a word that will remind you of your plan, and so on.

People interfering

- Use interpersonal skills to ask for their help. Ask them to reinforce you for using skills and ask them to stop engaging in behaviors that punish you.

- Use POS-itive thinking to help you understand your priorities. For example, be clear when your interpersonal purpose is more important than how the other feels about you.

MORE ON COMMITMENT

Since you've made it this far in reading this book, you've certainly made and kept a commitment to work on your bulimia. You may or may not have done every exercise, but you have likely made and kept a commitment to do at least some of the work. Commitment is an important step and it takes time and effort to do it well. It may be helpful to check in with your wise mind and be clear that the plan you've made to use these solutions is part of your purpose, as discussed in chapter 3. You might also want to go through the pros and cons of following through on your solutions.

Now make a private commitment directly to yourself to carry out your solutions the next time you encounter a prompting event. You can say silently to yourself, "I'm making a commitment to myself to carry out my plan." It helps some people to say this out loud or even write it down.

An additional step that helps many people is to make a public commitment. The public aspect of this act makes it more likely that you'll carry out a plan. Think of someone you trust, someone who can understand and will support you in changing your behavior. You don't have to tell them all the details of the solutions you've generated, but let them know a little bit about your plan. This may be a difficult thing to do, but consider doing everything you can to make it more likely that you'll follow through on the changes you want to make.

CONCLUSION

In this chapter, we looked at the steps for coming up with specific solutions for your bulimic behaviors and other related ineffective and problem behaviors. After determining solutions, we discussed how to troubleshoot those solutions and some things to do to develop and strengthen your commitment to following through. This was a long and detailed process, but it ensured that we could give you as much help as possible to develop solutions that will help you break the cycle of bulimia.

There is good news and bad news about this process. Because bulimia is a complex problem that's difficult to change, you most likely will have to repeat this process many times. Be patient with yourself, and find the willingness you need to do behavior and solution analysis over and over again. The good news is that each time you engage in the process, you'll learn more about your problem behaviors and what to do about them. This process can get easier and more effective over time. Reread chapter 3 if you need some help with staying motivated, and keep at the process of change. Keep track of times you successfully use skills, and encourage yourself as much as you can.

In the next two chapters we'll look at ways to handle relapse to problem behaviors. We'll also look at additional steps you can take if you need more help.

CHAPTER 10

Maintaining Healthy Eating and Coping with Relapse

Now that you've learned how to use the major components of DBT, how do you keep going even when you have urges to quit?

This chapter will help you develop a plan for maintaining the healthy eating patterns that you've established by working with this book. Relapse is a frequent occurrence with almost any change in behavior. With eating disorders, relapse is even considered a natural part of recovery. This chapter will help you learn how to cope with lapses, how to prevent lapses from developing into full-blown relapses, and how you can get back on track after relapse.

MAINTAINING HEALTHY EATING

The first thing that you must consider when trying to cope with relapse is the need to stick to healthy eating. If you recall from chapter 6, it is most healthy to eat something nutritionally well-balanced every three to four hours throughout the day. If you go longer than three or four hours without food, you aren't meeting your physiological needs, and you're increasing your sensitivity to emotions and emotional thinking. If you don't maintain healthy eating, you'll increase your vulnerability to Ed mind. After three or four hours of not eating, or not eating enough, your body will become hungry. Whether you experience this hunger as pronounced or not, when you finally do eat you're more likely to feel a loss of control and then binge. If you go for longer than four hours without eating, your mind will be constantly distracted from purposeful and effective thinking. Hunger will make you lose focus, and Ed will become all you can hear. It's crucial to first accept that you have an eating disorder so that you can then accept that relapse is a common component of recovery. When you accept that you have the possibility of relapse, you can be aware of when relapse occurs and label it as such. Only then can you make the healthier, more value-driven choice to return to healthy eating. Think about the third stanza of the poem by Portia Nelson, in chapter 3 "I still fall in…it's a habit…but, my eyes are open. I know where I am. It is *my* fault. I get out immediately" (1994, 3). Once you have become mindful of the relapse and the Ed-influenced eating, you will likely be more able to return to healthy eating and using the skills you've learned. It is essential to do both: use your skills *and* eat in a healthy manner. When you try to choose between using your skills or taking care of your physiological needs (especially healthy eating), it's like you're trying paddle upstream without oars. It makes reaching success much more difficult.

Brief Eating Assessment

Before we get into this chapter in earnest, let's take a look at your eating patterns right now. The information you gain here will help you work through the rest of the chapter.

How many times per day are you eating? _____

Have you eaten something nutritious in the last three to four hours?   _____ Yes   _____ No

Did you eat a healthy amount of food (not according to Ed mind but according to your wise mind)? _____ Yes   _____ No

When was the last time you went for more than three or four hours without eating? _____

What happened the next time you ate? _____

_____

Did you eat a healthy amount of food (not according to Ed mind but according to your wise mind)? _____ Yes   _____ No

Did you restrict?   _____ Yes   _____ No

Did you binge?   _____ Yes   _____ No

The more real nutritional knowledge you have, the better. It would be helpful to continue working with the food log from chapter 6. Seeing a nutritionist will also be effective. You may need to hear from a professional who is experienced with eating disorders (even a onetime visit) and who isn't influenced by Ed. When Ed starts talking, an expert opinion will help you distinguish between reality and what comes from Ed mind. Likewise, you must adjust your eating to your exercise habits. If you increase your exercise, your caloric intake must increase as well in order to keep your body functioning properly. For example, Michael Phelps had to eat 12,000 calories a day to keep his body performance at a high enough level to compete in the 2008 Olympics. While that's an extreme, you can see that you need to consider the situation when trying to find the appropriate and healthy physiological balance.

When you're struggling with bulimia, you may often experience an impulsive belief that your body doesn't need what everyone else needs. Ed will tell you that you shouldn't need to eat (as if eating were a sign of weakness). You don't have to believe those emotional thoughts, beliefs, interpretations, and myths. You can recognize them for what they are (simply emotional thoughts, beliefs, interpretations, and myths). Accept that you are human. As a human, you need to treat your body with respect in order to have a fulfilling life. You need to redirect your attention away from emotional, Ed-minded destructive thoughts, beliefs, interpretations, and myths.

Just as you need to respect your body's need for food, you also need to respect food itself. It's easy to see how food can viewed as bad or something threatening or scary when you have painfully struggled with food for so long. But food isn't the problem; it's necessary for survival. Part of the problem is your fear and judgment of food. You must remember that food nourishes you and keeps your body and mind functioning. If you continue to judge certain foods as good or bad, then food gets an immediate painful emotion attached to it. That judgment and the subsequent emotion prevent you from being able to have an objective and healthy attitude toward food. If you avoid all "bad" foods, inevitably you'll feel deprived. This deprivation often leads to bingeing. Bingeing further reinforces the growing belief that there are good and bad foods. So to maintain healthy eating, you need to be aware of your judgments. You must recognize that foods are not good or bad, they are simply more or less nutritionally balanced, and you need to eat a healthy, well-balanced diet to thrive.

COPING WITH RELAPSE

The rational part of your mind probably understands and agrees with the idea that it's important to maintain healthy eating patterns. And it's especially important to eat well when Ed mind kicks in and you have impulses to go back to old eating habits. When these impulses crop up, you can notice those thoughts and feelings and bring your attention back to the purpose of doing whatever you can to create a life worth being present in. If you are bargaining with or using Ed, you already know that you will likely feel worse as a result, which brings up even more reasons to use Ed to check out from your negative feelings. This doesn't help you progress to creating a life worth being present in.

So what do you do if you have a relapse? How do you cope without losing hope for recovery? You might sometimes feel hopeless or frustrated because you want the changes to occur overnight. You must remember that lasting change occurs slowly—but it *does* happen as long as you remain committed and willing to recommit when you slip. When trying to recover from bulimia, one of the big barriers is hopelessness. It is important to be mindful of hopelessness as an emotion. The intensity of this emotion can lead you to believe that your situation really is hopeless. It's so important that you can see this as emotion mind. When you can see hopelessness as an emotion and not as a fact about your life, then you can use skills to regulate that emotion and change your behavior.

For example, sometimes when Ellen was anxious due to things in life being a bit out of balance, she would have difficulty sleeping in the early morning. When she first began to learn mindfulness, she thought that counting her breaths would be an effective way to help her return to sleep when she had early morning awakenings around 4:00 AM. At first she would try to count her breaths, and at times she would get frustrated and feel hopeless that she wasn't falling asleep fast enough. With that frustration and hopelessness (resulting from a sleep-deprived, emotionally driven thought process), she would have thoughts like "It's just not working" or "I can't do this." She would then act on her thoughts as though they were truth and give up. As soon as she gave up, those thoughts really became truth—the mindfulness skill *didn't* work. This chain left her emotional and negative thoughts validated, proving to her that she really couldn't do it. Then one day as she was coaching someone else about DBT, she had a realization. She saw that when counting her breaths, she could simply notice her thoughts and feelings, even negative thoughts about failing at mindfulness, and let them pass through. Then she could bring her attention back to counting her breaths and continue the practice. The next time she woke up earlier than she wanted and had thoughts like "This will take forever," she realized that she could count her breaths until it was time to get up, if she had to. She remained committed to bringing her attention back to counting her breaths any time her attention wandered. She remained committed regardless of her hopeless emotion-driven thoughts. The next thing she knew, she was waking up to her alarm clock.

You can do this with recovery and relapse as well. You can simply *notice* thoughts like "DBT isn't working" or "I can't do this" and feelings of hopelessness. Then you can bring your attention back to your commitment to use your skills and do whatever you can to create a life worth being present in. If you give up because you think you can't do it, your notion becomes a self-fulfilling prophecy. This only leads to more hopelessness. Instead, you can redirect your attention and use your skills. Let's look at what Annie has to day about this process.

I keep having this Ed script that says, "You can stop after this episode" and so on. Ed has been saying this for years. I need to work on creating a response I can use when Ed jumps in with that one. Maybe I can just start to recognize the manipulation of it. Maybe it would go something like this:

Ed: You can binge and purge just this one time, and then I'll go away forever.

Annie: I don't even need to do this negotiation with you because I know what you're saying is false in every way. I am committed to not checking out.

Ed: But checking out helps! Don't you want to feel better? You can use your skills later—use me now.

Annie: Checking out helps only for a short amount of time, and I can't check out forever if I want to have a healthy life. I hear you calling me today, and I also know that you're a liar and a master manipulator. Our relationship isn't a healthy one. You need to get the hell out.

Annie notices the hole in the sidewalk and she chooses, in that moment, to step around the hole. She is aware that she's in an emotional state of mind, and she knows that she doesn't make healthy decisions when she's emotional (that would be stepping into the hole). She commits *in the moment* to not checking out, and she redirects her attention away from Ed-minded lies (stepping around the hole). It's important to remember that it isn't the lapse or relapse that keeps you from your purpose and from getting out of the hole; it's how you react to the lapse or relapse. If you give up, then the relapse continues and gets worse. If you accept the lapse or relapse by seeing it for what it is and problem solving, you will get out of the hole.

As you can see, when you act on your emotionally driven thoughts, it leads to consequences that only make it easier to believe them more the next time. If your belief in them is stronger, you're even more likely to act on them, which again leads you believe them even more. Eventually you've acted on them so much that you think you *know* that the thoughts are true. So what do you do when you have already begun to buy into emotionally driven thoughts and beliefs and are unintentionally turning them into fact by acting on them? You can write down the common Ed thoughts you're operating under to help you be more mindful of them when they pop up. You can then be aware enough to counter those thoughts and not act on them. The more often you are able to not act on those thoughts and beliefs, the more you can see that they aren't fact. The more you can see that they aren't fact, the more you'll be able to recognize how often those thoughts and beliefs weren't proven true.

Turning Thoughts into Facts

Take this opportunity to write down some of the Ed-mind thoughts or beliefs that often persuade you to act in unhelpful or unhealthy ways. If this feels unfamiliar, take a look at some of Annie's problem thoughts and beliefs, listed here:

1.   If I have one dessert food, I must binge on them all.

2.   If I go out to eat, I must get the smallest thing on the menu. Otherwise I'm just out of control.

3.   If I don't exercise, I'll binge and purge.

4.   If I don't follow my meal plan exactly, I must binge and purge.

5.   If I have a test to study for or a paper to write, I must binge to get through it.

6.   If I'm applying for a job, I must binge and purge to get through it.

7.   If there's tension in the house, I must check out.

8.   I shouldn't call someone for support because I should be able to do this on my own.

9.   If I try new food, I'll end up bingeing on it.

10.   If I'm not productive, I'll end up bingeing and purging.

      Now write your own:

1.   _____

2.   _____

3.   _____

4.   _____

5.   _____

6. _____

7. _____

8. _____

9. _____

10. _____

You can see how convincing some of these thoughts can be when you've had them, paid attention to them, and acted on them for so long. We suggest that you become aware of these thoughts and beliefs and use the skills you've learned and guidance from your wise mind to turn your attention away from them without acting on them.

Attention Naturally Drifts

It's important to keep in mind that because you are human, your attention naturally drifts to what might be judged as negatives. A leading expert on Japanese approaches to mental health, Gregg Krech, recognized that all attention naturally drifts toward less effective thoughts (2007). When this happens, you're more likely to get stuck in your emotionally driven Ed-minded thoughts. It will be helpful for you to be aware of this when it happens so that you can put in the effort to return your attention to a more effective focus.

Krech's table shows how attention tends to drift.

Attention Naturally Drifts

Toward	Away From
• My feelings and thoughts	• The present moment
• The past	• My environment
• The future	• What I am doing
• What other people should be doing	• The ways I am being supported
• My problems	• The troubles I am causing others
• Pain in my body	
• My needs and desires	

Copyright 2007 by Gregg Krech, ToDo Institute

As you can see, when your focus becomes stuck on your thoughts and feelings, fears about the future, and regrets about the past, you can't be aware of being in this present moment and your current environment. When your focus stays on what others should be doing differently or should be doing for you, you're stuck because you can't change others. It's much more effective to focus on what *you* are doing and what you can do differently to help yourself. Similarly, when your focus is stuck on your problems, pain in your body, or your needs and desires, you can't be mindful of the ways you're being supported by others or the way others sacrifice for you out of caring. Now do the following exercise to see what you're focused on and how that impacts your effectiveness.

Understanding How Your Attention Drifts

Write down your thoughts about each of these areas of attention.

What are your current feelings and thoughts?

_____

_____

What are you thinking about from the past? (This can be the recent past, like five minutes ago, or the remote past, like five years ago.)

_____

_____

What are you thinking about in the future? (This can be the near future or a more remote future.)

_____

_____

What do you think other people should be doing differently or doing for you?

_____

_____

What are the current problems you're focused on?

_____

_____

Do you have any pain in your body? If so, where is it and how much are you focused on it?

_____

_____

What are your current needs and desires?

_____

_____

Now that you can see some of the things that your attention naturally drifts toward, answer the following questions to see how you can pull your attention to a more productive and effective focus.

What's happening in this present moment and in your environment? Where are you? Focus on all of your senses. What do you see, what do you hear, what do you feel, and what do you smell?

_____

_____

_____

_____

What are you doing? What can you do to begin working on some of your problems? What skills can you use?

_____

_____

_____

_____

What are the ways you are being supported, and who is supporting you? Think about how others might be sacrificing for you because they care. Are you being supported at all financially? Even if you don't feel supported by someone, is there any chance that they are in fact offering you support, even if they're doing it in a way that isn't exactly what you need? (For example, you need to talk and they only feel comfortable showing support by giving money.)

_____

_____

So you can now recognize your Ed-minded thoughts and are aware and accepting of how your attention drift to a less effective focus, which is natural, because you're human. What might get in your way of coping with relapse? To be able to turn your attention away from Ed-mind thoughts and beliefs, you must be willing to put in the effort that would enable you to use your skills to do so.

How Do You Willfully Step in the Hole?

In Linehan's skills training manual (1993b) she discusses the difference between being willing and being willful. She describes willingness as doing what's needed to be effective by listening to your wise mind. She describes being willful as "doing nothing, giving up, doing the opposite of what works, trying to fix everything, and refusing to tolerate the moment" (177). Now check the ways that you tend to willfully step in the eating-disordered hole:

_____ Making decisions from an emotional state of mind

_____ Making decisions when sleep deprived

_____ Making decisions when restricting.

_____ Making decisions when _____

When making these decisions you buy into certain thoughts and beliefs and act as though they're true. If you act as though those thoughts and beliefs are based in truth, then they willfully become truth. Some examples of these thoughts or beliefs are below. Check those that apply to you:

_____ Refusing to believe that you can tolerate the moment

_____ Believing that you may as well give up fighting Ed now because you'll eventually give up anyway

_____ Believing that Ed is stronger than the healthy and wise you

_____ Other _____

As you can clearly see, acting on these self-destructive thoughts will only make them change from being just an emotionally driven thought to being fact.

If you can learn how you willfully step in the hole, then you can become more aware of it in the moment and more mindfully make a choice to not make any other decisions until you're back in wise mind. You can willingly redirect your attention back to using your skills instead of using your eating disorder.

But what happens if you learn the ways that you willfully step in the eating-disordered hole and then consciously and willfully make the decision to continue stepping in the hole? If that happens, you need to reexamine your commitment to recovery—to creating a life worth being present in, a life without your Ed mind constantly abusing you. You might even make a copy of the following exercise and post it prominently as a reminder or carry it around in your pocket to pull out when you need it. If the thought to use behaviors ever briefly crosses your mind, look at the following exercise.

Recommitting to Recovery

Answer the following questions:

Do you want to recover?   Yes _____   No _____

Do you want to create a life worth being present in?   Yes _____   No __

    If you answered yes to these questions, then it *must* start now, in this moment. It is a lie to believe that this is the last time you will use your problem behaviors. Every moment is a chance to commit and recommit. If you answered "no," examine which state of mind you are in and use your skill to get back to wise mind.

    You're more likely to become steadfastly willful when in emotion mind or rational mind, but not in wise mind. If you find yourself in this place, ask yourself how that's working for you.

    You're also more likely to become willful about your eating disorder when in distress. This distress can be about something totally unrelated or even about not wanting to accept that you even have an eating disorder. Recall from chapter 7 that all people have four basic options when in distress:

1. Problem solve the situation.

2. Change your interpretation or how you feel about the situation.

3. Do nothing different and stay just as miserable as you are now.

4. Radically accept what you cannot change and go back to problem solving about what you can change.

    Problem solving the distress would mean practicing your newly developed DBT skills regularly so that when you need them they'll be familiar and effective. Changing your interpretation of the situation means recognizing how your current interpretation is feeding Ed, then thinking about the many other possible interpretations. If you are so intertwined with Ed mind that you can't generate other interpretations, then begin by just thinking about off-the-wall ideas. You can even start with thinking of things that sound totally silly, like "space aliens came down to earth to make this happen." Once you begin thinking of enough silly ideas, then some more realistic ideas might begin to occur to you too. For example, if you're distressed because you have an eating disorder, you can change your interpretation by recognizing that you have an eating disorder, that it isn't your fault and doesn't make you bad—it simply is what it is, and you can learn skills to not engage in your eating disorder. We know that falling or even jumping into that hole is doing nothing different and means staying in misery. The fourth option is to radically accept what you cannot change (that you have an eating disorder) and work toward changing what you can (learning and practicing new skills so that you don't engage in your eating disorder).

CONCLUSION

In this chapter you learned how to develop a plan for maintaining more healthy eating patterns, and you have seen some obstacles that can arise. You now understand that relapse is a frequent occurrence with change in behavior, and it's even considered part of the process of recovery from eating disorders. Now, you can be more aware of thoughts and beliefs that can become self-fulfilling prophecies, and you can recognize your naturally drifting attention and make efforts to redirect it. By doing these things, you can maintain your commitment to using your DBT skills and to doing whatever is necessary to create a life worth being present in. And you can do it over and over again.

CHAPTER 11

Bringing It All Together

As you come to the end of this workbook, it's important to remember that the skills you've learned *must be practiced*. If you don't practice them regularly enough to make them very familiar, you won't even think to use them when you really need the help. In this workbook you've learned about bulimia and how dialectical behavioral therapy can be an effective way to create a life worth being present in. You have come to understand bulimia and its symptoms. In the introduction to DBT, you became familiar with the central dialectic of acceptance and change, the role of emotion regulation in problem eating, and some of the research conducted on this form of therapy. You learned how to assess your readiness for change and then to take action through Morita and Naikan therapies. In this process, you have found your motivation or purpose, and you understand that it's most effective to recommit to this purpose moment by moment. You have found the effectiveness of shifting your attention from your thoughts and feelings to a focus on your purpose-driven intention. Identifying and understanding your patterns through the process of behavior analysis has enabled you to identify patterns of events and behaviors that support and maintain your problematic eating.

Throughout this workbook, you have learned many DBT skills. You have acquired skills that enable you to learn how to be present in the moment and without judgment, skills to understand and more objectively evaluate your emotions, and skills to regulate your emotions. You now know how to tolerate distress when there's nothing you can do about it in the moment, resisting checking out with bulimic behaviors. Additionally, you've learned how to interact with others more effectively so you don't feel driven to escape with bulimic behaviors when facing interpersonal problems. You can now use behavioral skills to break the maladaptive patterns of behavior that lead to your disordered eating. Finally, you've learned how to maintain healthy eating habits, how to cope with the expected relapses, and how to get back on track after relapse.

As you can see in this e-mail our client Sharon wrote to a friend, she has much of what she learned together:

DBT has given me tools, in conjunction with the tools of AA, to communicate my feelings more effectively rather than numbing them with food. DBT has also taught me how to meditate more effectively throughout the day and how to regulate my emotions. It has also given me the ability to sit through the most uncomfortable/painful times (like when I want to rip my skin off) with distress tolerance skills.

Lately, before I binge/purge or am at the "screw it" point, I'm more likely to ask myself, "Will this help me create a life worth being present in?" I don't always ask the question, but when I remember to ask, it has helped. I try to distract myself from the idea and the feelings of needing to binge/purge by doing the next right thing—the very thing in front of me. I'm finding it really interesting, now that I'm further into recovery, how much this food stuff turns out to be a distraction from what I'm really feeling/doing/thinking/obsessing about.

Now that Sharon has been awakened from her bulimic nightmare, she can see how her bulimic behaviors tended to be self-perpetuating—one leading into and feeding the next. As you can see from her e-mail, she puts all the skills together and recognizes that there are different times for her to use different skills. She also knows that each of the skills is important.

CREATING YOUR PRACTICE PLAN

You can see that getting practice is crucial, so make sure that you practice at least one skill every day. With this in mind, let's go ahead and create a plan that will let you know which skills you'll be practicing for each day of the week.

First, let's address your mindfulness practice. Mindfulness and taking a nonjudgmental stance can be so unfamiliar that these skills need to be practiced daily to be effective when needed. The way you should integrate mindfulness into your practice is to spend a few minutes each day intentionally practicing mindfulness of your breath. It will work best if you can make this a routine for yourself, practicing at the same time each day. Take time, at least five minutes every day, to be purposefully mindful. You can simple be aware, nonjudgmentally and one-pointedly of what you do for five minutes. Or you can use one of the mindfulness practice exercises you learned in chapter 5.

Once you have decided how you'll practice mindfulness, you need to plan for how you'll practice the other DBT skills. When creating your practice plan, come up with at least one other skill to practice every day along with your daily mindfulness practice. You must keep practicing, so it's best to make a concrete plan to help support you in this goal. You must practice, and you must plan for it. Use the following practice plan to help you keep track of your practice. Start by going through the practices in each chapter again, systematically. Once the skills become more familiar, you can begin to notice that you're practicing the skills without conscious effort. In addition to practicing in this organized way, definitely use any skills you need to help you with situations in your daily life. As the skills become more familiar you'll see that you practice the skills as you move through each day. As you notice that, you can simply keep track of your practice on the form so that you see how often you're practicing the skills without effort.

Mindfulness

- Noticing

- Labeling

- Engaging

- Using equanimity

- Doing one thing at a time

- Acting effectively

- Entering wise mind

Emotion Regulation

- Interpreting your emotions

- Taking a mindful moment

- Getting to know your emotions

- Attending to physiological balance

    - Eating

    - Sleep

    - Illness or pain

    - Substances

- Skills to regulate your emotions

    - Evaluating the validity of emotions

    - Mindfulness of emotions

    - Awareness of worry thoughts

    - Experiencing short-term positives

    - Building long-term positives

    - Breaking down goals into steps toward long-term positives

    - Doing the opposite of emotionally motivated urges

Distress Tolerance

- Being the BOSS of distraction

  - Focusing on being busy

  - Focusing on others

  - Focusing on strong sensations

  - Focusing on statements of self-support

- Learning to soothe yourself with sounds, sight, smell, and touch

- Tolerating distress by finding another focus

- Tolerating distress by focusing on values

- Tolerating distress by focusing on being present in the moment

- Radical acceptance

Interpersonal Skills

- Finding balance

  - No woe

- POS-itive thinking

  - What is your purpose?

  - How you want the other to feel about you

  - How you want to feel about yourself

- Interpersonal purpose skills

  - Assertiveness skills

    - Explaining

    - Asserting

    - Rewarding

- Response skills

  - Confidence

  - Persistence

  - Fogging

  - Negotiating

- Other relationship skills

  - Active listening

    - Expressing feelings of concern

  - Building and maintaining relationship with yourself

PRACTICE PLAN

Monday	Tuesday	Wednesday	Thursday	Friday	Saturday	Sunday
Monday Practice mindfulness and taking a nonjudgmental stance	**Tuesday** Practice mindfulness and taking a nonjudgmental stance	**Wednesday** Practice mindfulness and taking a nonjudgmental stance	**Thursday** Practice mindfulness and taking a nonjudgmental stance	**Friday** Practice mindfulness and taking a nonjudgmental stance	**Saturday** Practice mindfulness and taking a nonjudgmental stance	**Sunday** Practice mindfulness and taking a nonjudgmental stance
Skills to practice	Skills to practice	Skills to practice	Skills to practice	Skills to practice	Skills to practice	Skills to practice

Now that you have a solid practice plan, it's equally important that you have a plan for what you'll do when in emotional distress or when emotionally dysregulated. Then, when you experience these strong emotions and have the impulse to check out with your bulimic behaviors, you can turn to your action plan and immediately see that you have other choices.

Action Plan

What stage of readiness are you in? (See chapter 3 for information on the stages of change.)

_____

What is your purpose?

_____

_____

What will you do when you realize you are in emotion mind?

_____

Which mindfulness exercises will you do to help you return to wise mind?

_____

_____

Have you looked at your behavioral patterns and are you aware of your ineffective behaviors?

_____

_____

What can you do differently next time?

_____

_____

When in emotion mind, what skills will you use?

_____

_____

When you're in distress and can't change the situation, how will you tolerate the distress without making things worse?

_____

_____

When having interpersonal problems, what skills will you use?

_____

_____

When you relapse, how will you get back on track?

_____

_____

Use this action plan as a reminder of your options when you are in emotional distress and you're not thinking clearly and wisely.

HOW TO GET FURTHER HELP

If you have completed this workbook and you continue to struggle with bulimia or bulimic behaviors, it's very important that you seek professional help, even if simply to get a professional assessment. For more information on dialectical behavioral therapy and how to find therapists who practice DBT, you can go to the website www.behavioraltech.org. For more information about how to find a therapist who specializes in eating disorders, you can check out the following websites: Eating Disorder Referral and Information Center at www.edreferral.com, www.something-fishy.org, or the National Eating disorders Association at www.nationaleatingdisorders.org.

CONCLUSION

We understand that using DBT to help in your struggle with bulimia is no easy task. It requires great commitment, time, and effort. While we know that the road ahead can be anxiety provoking, we are equally sure that it's worth doing. Think about all of the commitment, time, and effort that you currently give to Ed. If you just take that amount of energy and use it to master DBT skills, your eating disorder and recovery will eventually require less and less time and effort in your life. You will have a life worth being present in, and you will no longer be spending your time and effort with Ed. In reading this book, taking the time to learn the concepts and skills, and working to apply them in your life, you have made major steps forward in your efforts to take charge of your bulimia and other problems in your life. This has undoubtedly been hard work already. Most likely there will also be a lot of challenging work ahead. Keep at it, and your efforts will be rewarded. Acknowledge your discouragement over any setbacks that occur, and use your skills to keep going. You can do it!

References

American Psychiatric Association. 2000. *Diagnostic and Statistical Manual of Mental Disorders*. 4th ed. (text revision). Washington DC: American Psychiatric Association.

Bower, G., and S. Bower. 1980. *Asserting Yourself: A Practical Guide for Positive Change*. Reading, MA: Addison-Wesley.

Bulik, C.M., P.F. Sullivan, and K.S. Kendler. 1998. Heritability of binge-eating and broadly defined bulimia nervosa. *Biological Psychiatry* 44(12):1210-1218.

Csíkszentmihályi, M. 1990. *Flow: The Psychology of Optimal Experience*. New York: Harper and Row

Fitzgibbon, M.L., L.A. Sánchez-Johnsen, and Z. Martinovich. 2003. A test of the continuity perspective across bulimic and binge eating pathology. *International Journal of Eating Disorders* 34(1):83–97.

Gambrill, E.D., and C. Richey. 1985. *Taking Charge of Your Social Life*. Belmont, CA: Wadsworth.

Germer, C.K., R.D. Siegel, and P.F. Fulton. 2005. *Mindfulness and Psychotherapy*. New York: Guilford Press.

Goleman, D. 1988. *The Meditative Mind: The Varieties of Meditative Experience*. New York: Putnam Pubishing Group.

Gunaratana, B.H. 2002. *Mindfulness in Plain English*. Somerville, MA: Wisdom Publications.

Harlow, H. 1958. The nature of love. *American Psychologist* 13:673-685.

Krech, G. 2002. *Naikan: Gratitude, Grace, and the Japanese Art of Self-Reflection*. Berkeley, CA: Stone Bridge Press.

Krech, G. 2007. A Natural Approach to Mental Wellness. Monkton, VT: ToDo Institute.

Linehan, M.M. 1993a. *Cognitive-Behavioral Treatment of Borderline Personality Disorder.* New York: Guilford Press.

Linehan, M.M. 1993b. *Skills Training Manual for Treating Borderline Personality Disorder.* New York: Guilford Press.

Linehan, M.M. 2005. Advances in Emotion Regulation. Address at the 21st Annual Cape Cod Symposia, Cape Cod, MA.

Marlatt, G.A., and J.R. Gordon. 1985. *Relapse Prevention: Maintenance Strategies in the Treatment of Addictive Behaviors.* New York: Guilford Press.

Morita S., M. Morita, A. Kondo, and P. LeVine. 1998. *Morita Therapy and the True Nature of Anxiety-Based Disorders (Shineishitsu).* New York: SUNY Press

Nelson, P. 1993. *There's a Hole in My Sidewalk.* Hillsboro, OR: Beyond Words Publishing.

Nhat Hanh, T. 1975. *The Miracle of Mindfulness: An Introduction to the Practice of Meditation.* Boston: Beacon Press.

Prochaska, J.O., and C.C. DiClemente. 1983. Stages and processes of self-change of smoking: Toward an integrative model of change. *Journal of Consulting and Clinical Psychology* 51(3):390-395.

Rosen, C. 2008. The myth of multitasking. *The New Atlantis: A Journal of Technology and Science,* Spring, 105-110.

Safer, D.L., C.F. Telch, and W.S. Agras. 2001. Dialectical behavior therapy for bulimia nervosa. *American Journal of Psychiatry* 158(4):632-634

Schafer, J., with T. Rutledge. 2004. *Life Without Ed: How One Woman Declared Independence from Her Eating Disorder and How You Can Too.* New York: McGraw-Hill.

Smith, M. J. 1975. *When I Say No, I Feel Guilty.* New York: Bantam Books.

Telch, C.F., W.S. Agras, and M.M. Linehan. 2001. Dialectical behavior therapy for binge eating disorder. *Journal of Consulting and Clinical Psychology* 69(6):1061-1065.

Ellen Astrachan-Fletcher, Ph.D., is founder and director of the eating disorders clinic at the University of Illinois Medical Center, where she is also an associate professor. She has over ten years of clinical experience as a licensed clinical psychologist, specializing in eating disorders and women's mental health issues. She is a member of the American Psychological Association and the Academy for Eating Disorders.

Michael Maslar, Psy.D., is founder and director of the Mindfulness and Behavior Therapies Program at The Family Institute at Northwestern University. He is also an assistant professor at Northwestern University Medical School in Chicago, IL. Maslar has extensive training in dialectical behavior therapy (DBT) and is a member of the American Psychological Association and the Association for Behavioral and Cognitive Therapies.

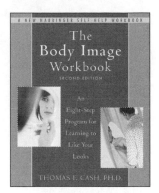